Writers of Wales

EDITORS

MEIC STEPHENS   R. BRINLEY JONES

1. The Arch Druid.   2. Proclaiming the London Eisteddfod.
3. Pennillion singing.   4. Sounding the Bugle.
5. Defending the Institution of the Eisteddfod.

Proclaiming the National Eisteddfod of 1887
in the Temple Gardens, London.

Hywel Teifi Edwards

THE
EISTEDDFOD

University of Wales Press
on behalf of the Welsh Arts Council

1990

I

There is a story that tells of a sixth-century eisteddfod held in Conway at the royal behest of Maelgwn Gwynedd. It was his wish that the assembled bards and minstrels should compete against each other, but first they would have to swim across the river, the minstrels bearing their harps on their backs. Having thus, with characteristic cunning, effectively nullified the opposition, his favourites, the bards, naturally scooped the pot. Such a story deserves to be true. For the purpose of this work it places literature at the heart of the eisteddfod tradition and it points to the shady side of competition which has gleefully preoccupied commentators throughout the ages. Moreover, it encapsulates one truth about the eisteddfod for which proof abounds. It has always provided a lively, occasionally outrageous, context for an appreciation of the arts in Welsh life.

This narrative essay should not be confused with an outline history of an institution which dates (at least) from 1176. It will have most to say about the National Eisteddfod and the factors determining the nature of the literature it has produced from the 1860s down to the present

1

day. The second half of the nineteenth century witnessed an explosion of eisteddfod activity at local, regional and national levels, and the effects of that activity have still to be recorded, let alone appreciated. The Victorian Welshman chose to be observed and inspected in the eisteddfod arena. By means of this singular institution he sought recognition and acceptance at home and abroad. For it he created a huge, striving body of literature, often clamant with an anxiety masquerading as self-congratulation, in which his descendants today can find invaluable evidence of the stresses and strains of Welshness during a fateful stage in its evolution.

How the National Eisteddfod came to dominate the Welsh cultural scene during the Victorian heyday, and how a multitude of feeder eisteddfodau afforded thousands of ordinary people a means of self-expression, lies outside the scope of this essay. Likewise, the impact of twentieth-century higher education on standards and the many demands which the continuing and deepening crisis of Welshness has made on the institution throughout this century can only be touched upon here. Suffice it to say that a remarkable story waits to be told and one can only hope that if the Departments of Welsh within our University survive the depredations of Thatcherism, they will give federal thanks by adopting the National Eisteddfod as a prime research project which will give issue to a number of detailed studies. The powers that be, once assured of its strong American connection, would surely be happy to back it!

The year 1789 marks the beginning of the modern eisteddfod. Its development as a popular institution, as an agency for quickening a public interest in literature and music, dates from the positive response made by the Gwyneddigion Society in London to the promptings of Thomas Jones, an exciseman from Corwen whose disenchantment with the irregular, beery eisteddfodau of eighteenth-century Wales drove him to action following a dismal meeting in Llangollen in January, 1789, when old Jonathan Hughes (1721–1805) and his son succeeded in attracting two other poets to join with them in another eisteddfod which purported to maintain the tradition intact.

Thomas Jones realized that there was little hope of regeneration from within Wales, given the Anglicized condition of the gentry who alone had the means to promote a serious concern with the arts. But in London there were a number of relatively prosperous Welsh exiles who retained an affection for their homeland, including a minority who took an enthusiastic and informed interest in its culture. The Honourable Society of Cymmrodorion, established in 1751, followed a rather uneven course before coming to a halt in 1787. In the mean time, a breakaway group of malcontents mostly from north Wales had formed the Gwyneddigion Society in 1770 to foster a more committed approach to the promotion of Welsh culture, and it was to the recorder of this Society, William Owen-Pughe (1759–1835), that Thomas Jones addressed his plea for help in 1789, thereby inaugurating a new era in the history of the eisteddfod.

Before proceeding further let us remind our-
selves that the noun 'eisteddfod' derives from
the verb 'eistedd' (to sit) and literally means a
'sitting together', a session (probably competitive
from its inception) of bards and minstrels intent
on exercising and advancing their particular
crafts in the presence of a distinguished patron.
It must surely have evolved within the bardic
system that fostered a tradition of praise poetry
composed by professionally trained bards long
before 1176 when Lord Rhys of Deheubarth, as
we are told in BRUT Y TYWYSOGION (*The Chronicle
of the Princes*), held an eisteddfod at Cardigan
Castle at Christmastide. What few details the
BRUT offers encourage the view that it could not
have been the first of its kind, but this essay
affords no room for further speculation.

It is necessary, however, to recount briefly what
happened in three eisteddfodau held at Carmarthen, circa 1450 and Caerwys in 1523 and 1567.
These tell us a great deal about the contemporary concerns of the Welsh bards and the
'official' response to them, a response that was
to greatly influence the conception which
eighteenth-century eisteddfodwyr had of the
way a revived institution should serve poetry.

The Carmarthen eisteddfod, which according to
one chronicler lasted for three months(!), was
presided over by Gruffudd ap Nicolas (*fl.* 1425–
56), the most powerful *uchelwr* in south Wales by
the middle of the century and himself, in all
probability, a competent bard who was driven
not only by a wish to emulate Lord Rhys, but by
a desire to strengthen and enhance the tradition

4

with which he identified. Put simply, he sought through the eisteddfod to secure the status of the professional bards and, in keeping with what had happened in England during the previous century, to protect them from the trespass of hacks and impostors who inflicted themselves on the populace to their cost. That perennial urge to reform and regulate, which still shows no sign of abating, dominated the Carmarthen eisteddfod, and the labours of one man in particular were to determine the cut of strict-metre poetry down to this century.

The 'Cadair Arian' (*Silver Chair*) said to have been fashioned by Gruffudd ap Nicolas himself, was won by a bard who came from Hanmer, in Flintshire. Dafydd ab Edmwnt (*fl.* 1450–97) was an *uchelwr* who did not depend on patronage. He was in every other respect a professional bard who was highly regarded by his fellows and who, after the Carmarthen eisteddfod, was to be hailed as a reforming defender of the bardic tradition.

Far more important than his winning *cywydd* in praise of the Trinity was his revision and winnowing of the strict metres and the *cynganeddion*, – the source materials of those core subjects taught to students in the bardic schools. The traditional knowledge imparted in them was incorporated in the 'Grammars' of the chief bards (*Gramadegau'r Penceirddiaid*), standard text-books bearing the imprint of two fourteenth-century ecclesiasts, Einion Offeiriad from Gwynedd and Dafydd Ddu Athro from Hiraddug. It was Dafydd ab Edmwnt's purpose to maintain the integrity of the bardic tradition by making more complex and intricate those rules and metrical devices which were intended in the first place to safeguard a hermetic art by keeping the uninitiated in their proper place – on the outside.

Without going into detail it can be said that he reinforced a predilection for rhetorical display and technical difficulty which had long characterized Welsh poetry. The changes he made, as contained in the 'Grammar' compiled by his disciple, Gutun Owain, were to confront Welsh poets with fear-induced constraints for generations to come, and an increasingly mechanical application of his criteria was to bedevil strict-metre poetry from the seventeenth century onwards as the tradition which had given rise to them disintegrated. From the literary upsurge of the eighteenth century and throughout the nineteenth, poets and critics would have much to say about Dafydd ab Edmwnt's reforms, but it would take a John Morris-Jones (1864–1929) to make the debate bear fruit. Nevertheless, ab Edmwnt retained his hold on the Chair competition in this century as well and from 1938–64 the National Eisteddfod specifically asked for an *awdl* that would be a compound of as many of the revised strict metres as the poet chose to use. Dafydd ab Edmwnt is truly synonymous with that concern for past practice which is a constant in the eisteddfod story.

By the middle of the sixteenth century, however, the decline in the bardic tradition was well advanced. Loss of patronage coupled with the threat posed by an increasing army of vagabonds and bunglers clearly underlined the need for something to be done. The professionals would have to reassert their authority. Without official recognition of their skills they would find themselves face to face with a hostile society tired of being imposed upon by dubious vagrants and sturdy beggars that the law now required should be put to honest work. The famous Caerwys eisteddfodau of 1523 and 1567 were got up with the active support of the famous Mostyn family to licence genuine bards and minstrels. It was as if a clinic was being provided for the examination of ailing professionals from which no one whose fitness was in doubt would emerge with a clean bill of health.

The proclamation of the 1523 eisteddfod emphasized that its prime purpose was to regulate and correct bardic practices in accordance with the Statute of Gruffudd ap Cynan, a king of Gwynedd (c. 1055–1137) reputed to have supported an eisteddfod in Caerwys in his own day. What most mattered was that the standard of excellence of past and aspiring graduates should be fully confirmed. It is no longer accepted that the Statute bearing his name was the work of Gruffudd ap Cynan. It probably dates from the early sixteenth century, Gruffudd ap Cynan's name having been appropriated to give the Statute the authoritative stamp of a historical figure who, it was believed, reformed the bardic system in Wales along the lines of the Irish tradition with which he had familiarized himself during his exile in Dublin.

What matters to us now is the way in which the Statute reflects the crisis to which it addressed itself, laying great stress on the competence of the bards and minstrels, loudly proclaiming their rights as a privileged fraternity and insisting on a code of conduct that would at all times be consonant with the nobility of their calling. Drunkenness, womanizing and gambling were even then singled out for censure, long before the Nonconformist thumpers of nineteenth-century Wales got the bit between their teeth. Put simply, the Statute of Gruffudd ap Cynan crystallized the rationale of the bardic system at a time when the old order seemed more and more at risk. It reaffirmed the canons of classical praise poetry which demanded that the bard celebrate in elevated language the orderliness of a God-centred world.

None the less, by 1567 further restorative action was required and the second Caerwys eisteddfod was held 'by the commission of the grace of the queen and her councillors', – councillors being members of the Council of Wales and the Marches. No less a person than William Salesbury sent its promoters a copy of Gruffudd ap Cynan's Statute, urging them to alter or revise as they saw it *befitting or unbefitting to the present age.* The 1567 eisteddfod was meant to confirm the Statute together with the resolutions of the 1523 eisteddfod, and since a number of the gentlemen who supported it were Justices of the Peace they were well placed to tackle all those *sturdy and idle vagabonds* who might presume to appear before them in the guise of true bards. Should they fail to qualify for the appropriate 'degrees' that testified to a bard's fitness for his role they would be put to some honest work. Like today's abusers of the

Social Security system they were to be called to account and penalized, whereas the genuine practitioners, who had been *much discouraged to travail in the exercise and practice of their knowledges and also not a little hindered in their livings and preferments,* would be encouraged and their worth recognized.

It is regrettable that what poetry was produced for these early eisteddfodau is lost to us, neither have we anything in the way of criticism to learn from. But we need not doubt its conservatism. It would most certainly be rooted in standard practice. Originality would mean no more than permutating stock devices and timeworn motifs, images and symbols within structures that proved very resistant to change. The kind of enlightened criticism that could have given the bards a more adventurous role was kept at arm's length. Welsh humanists, whose minds and imaginations had been enlivened by Renaissance learning, longed to confront the bardic system with the challenge of a new world, to make it more accessible to modern influences.

William Salesbury (c. 1520–84), Siôn Dafydd Rhys (1534–c. 1619) and Gruffudd Robert (c. 1532–98) are notable examples of humanist scholars who lamented the 'closed shop' mentality of the bards. Their obsessive defence of trade secrets immured them in a past that denied them a meaningful future. Furthermore, their unquestioning perpetuation of praise poetry distanced them from that concern with the truth about life which lay at the heart of the 'new learning'. Their praise was often too easily bought, a charge which Siôn Tudur (c. 1522–1602), echoing the

9

famous Sion Cent (*c.* 1400–30/45), was to make in a *cywydd* addressed to his fellow-bards.

In a notable exchange of *cywyddau* which lasted for seven years (1580–87/8) between Wiliam Cynwal, a professional bard and Edmwnd Prys, a former university man, then Archdeacon of Merioneth, Prys tried unavailingly to win Cynwal over to the humanist standpoint. He wanted the bards 'I roi gwir ar y gorau' (*To put forth truth at its best*). Cynwal in reply taunted him with his ignorance of the bardic tradition and his defective verse, 'Byr d'addysg ar brydyddiaeth' (*Your bardic education falls short*). And that was that. The professional bard, content with his lot, was determined to go his own way and that convergence of literary interests which could have resulted in a new flowering of Welsh poetry was forestalled.

In 1701 an eisteddfod was held at Machynlleth *To begin to renew, and put in order the Eisteddfod of Bards* (as they were in old times), to *reprimand false* '*cynghanedd*', *to explain the difficult and intricate things, and to confirm what is correct in the art of poetry in the Welsh language*. There followed, throughout the century, a number of 'Eisteddfodau'r Almanaciau', so called because they were advertised in the cheap and popular almanacks that circulated widely at that time. They never amounted to much, hardly ever attracted more than a fistful of poets and minstrels, and produced at best a clutch of commonplace, extempore *englynion* and *cywyddau* in praise of local worthies that owed more to the beery atmosphere in which they were composed than to genuine inspiration and craft.

Their promoters, however, fervently hoped that they would serve to revive the fortunes of Welsh literature. They were seen by them as being in direct descent from the Caerwys eisteddfodau, and one man in particular, Siôn Rhydderch (1673–1735), poet and printer, was much concerned to ensure their success. In 1728 he published a 'Grammar' which restated the ideals of the past, based quite obviously on the Statute of Gruffudd ap Cynan. The poets of the day were to reject those debased forms of poetry which the mastercraftsmen of old had rejected, there being no rules to govern them. They should confine themselves to the twenty-four strict metres and entrust their art to the adjudication of an acknowledged master, or masters – for Siôn Rhydderch was prepared to countenance a juridical bench of twelve!

But there was to be no return to former glories. In 1734, shortly before his death, he journeyed to Dolgellau and found there some half a dozen poets and all the signs of apathy and dejection. Harking back to what seemed to him, in comparison, the splendour of the 1567 eisteddfod he concluded that he was labouring in vain. He would no more trouble himself with eisteddfodau ... *unless some others may feel like restarting and setting up the thing. And if it will be like that, if I am alive and well, I shall not be hindered from coming to that.* Fifty-five years later, Thomas Jones approached the Gwyneddigion and the eisteddfod took off on a course undreamt of by Siôn Rhydderch.

Thomas Jones added his voice to that of Jonathan Hughes who had asked the Gwyneddigion for their patronage, *some small present out of goodwill to those who are trying to crawl after their mother tongue* . . . The Gwyneddigion saw fit to respond positively but, and it is a significant but in view of the eisteddfod's subsequent development, their offer of support was not unconditional. The Society claimed the right in future to proclaim the eisteddfod, together with the subject of the main competition which they alone would set, a year in advance. Poems would be submitted pseudonymously, the adjudicators would decide on their merits and then forward them, together with their adjudications, in a sealed package to the eisteddfod. The adjudicators would be fit men for their task and should consider *purity of Language and regular composition of the Poems to be among their chief merits.* They should meet to give an impartial adjudication, and in the event of any disagreement the Gwyneddigion would undertake to resolve it. On the first day of the eisteddfod the name of the victorious poet would be announced and with due regard to his status as *pencerdd* he would not compete with the other poets in the composition of impromptu verse.

Here, then, we have the blueprint for the National Eisteddfod. There was to be notice given a year in advance of *one* organized, annual eisteddfod answerable to a central, controlling authority which would require competitors to submit their compositions pseudonymously to a panel of competent adjudicators.

What most concerns us now, however, is the

Gwyneddigion's insistence on the paramountcy of the long poem. They aimed to turn the eisteddfod into an Academy that would act as a forcing house for Welsh culture. They were not to succeed in that respect, but they did bring into being the kind of *awdl* that, together with the *pryddest*, would dominate the poetry of the modern eisteddfod. Prior to 1789 the poets, misled by the examples contained in Siôn Rhydderch's 'Grammar', had concocted 'awdlau enghreifftiol' *(exemplars)* which demanded the deployment of all the strict metres. As we now know, they took for their models those 'exercises' which the bardic schools had once required of their students, and the results are best left to the imagination.

Basing their conception of a fitting *awdl* on the experience of the poet they venerated, the Revd Goronwy Owen (1723–69), the Gwyneddigion urged the poets to *choose* those strict metres that best suited their artistic purposes. Goronwy Owen's ambition to write a Welsh Miltonic, Christian epic had been frustrated by the inadequacy of the twenty-four strict metres, and his studied comments on the intractable nature of some of them carried much weight with his admirers.

The *awdlau* written for the Bala eisteddfod of September 1789 on the set subject, 'Ystyriaeth ar Oes Dyn' *(A Consideration of Man's Life)*, heralded the appearance of the new *awdl*. Its predominance was assured by Dafydd Ddu Eryri (David Thomas, 1759–1822) and the young poets he nurtured, and by the middle of the nineteenth century such

13

awdlau as 'Elusengarwch' (*Charity*), 1819, by Dewi Wyn o Eifion (Dewi Owen, 1784–1841); 'Dinystr Jerusalem' (*The Destruction of Jerusalem*), 1824, by Eben Fardd (Ebenezer Thomas, 1802–63) and 'Drylliad y *Rothesay Castle*' (*The Wreck of the 'Rothesay Castle'*), 1832, by Caledfryn (the Revd William Williams, 1801–69) were adduced as proof that contemporary poetry excelled by far all that had gone before. The practice, by now familiar, of 'chairing' the successful *awdlwr* which began in the early 1790s merely served to 'authenticate' the art he practised by symbolizing the ancient tradition to which he belonged.

If the Gwyneddigion had thought to rid the eisteddfod of discord they were soon disabused. Although not actively involved in the Corwen eisteddfod in May 1789 – Thomas Jones simply used their name for promotional purposes – they were dragged into the bitter altercation that ensued when Gwallter Mechain (the Revd Walter Davies, 1761–1849) was adjudged the winner, having been told in advance by none other than Thomas Jones of the subjects intended for impromptu treatment. Despite the vociferous support for Jonathan Hughes and Twm o'r Nant (Thomas Edwards, 1738–1810), the Gwyneddigion upheld the decision and did the same in September when Gwallter Mechain's successful *awdl*, again composed with the benefit of inside information provided by Owain Myfyr, the Society's mainstay, aroused further controversy at Bala.

We can, at least, respect their courage bearing in mind that a fiery champion of Twm o'r Nant, a one-time naval surgeon by the name of Dafydd

Samwel who sailed with Captain Cook on his last voyage, was ever ready to settle differences with a duel. Perhaps this kind of man, *tall, stout, black-haired, pock-marked, fierce-looking, wondrous friendly in company and very fond of the cup* should always be on hand to test an adjudicator's resolve. As for Gwallter Mechain, the reverend gentleman certainly took winning seriously and he was still striving shortly before his death in 1849 when, according to an acquaintance, he was in his dotage. He was probably the first of that horde of incurable competitors that the revived eisteddfod was to breed after 1789.

The Napoleonic wars brought the Gwyneddigion initiative to a halt, but the eisteddfod movement was reactivated in 1818 when a fraternity of clerics inspired by Ifor Ceri (the Revd John Jenkins, 1770–1829), vicar of Kerry in Montgomeryshire, set up 'The Cambrian Society in Dyfed' to work for *the preservation of Ancient British Literature, poetical, historical, antiquarian, sacred and moral and the encouragement of national music.* Similar societies were quickly established in Gwynedd (1819), Powys (1819), Gwent and Morgannwg (1821) and this structure was then capped by the reappearance in 1820 of 'The Cymmrodorion Society, or the Metropolitan Cambrian Institute' which was to act as a central authority guiding and co-ordinating the efforts of the societies in Wales.

Ten 'Provincial Eisteddfodau' were held between 1819–34, eisteddfodau of a kind and on a scale never witnessed before. They were patronized by an Anglicized gentry and graced by royalty when George IV's brother, the Duke of Sussex, appeared at Denbigh in 1828 to be followed at Beaumaris in 1832 by the young Princess Victoria and her mother. But they did not realize Ifor Ceri's ambitions. They did little to help catalogue and assemble at some place accessible to scholars as many of those manuscripts central to Welsh learning (or dependable copies of them) as could be found in Britain and Europe. They did little to forward the cause of that National Library long since mooted by the Cymmrodorion and the Gwyneddigion. The 'Provincial Eisteddfodau' fell a prey to the concerts introduced by Bardd Alaw (John Parry, 1776–1851) in which expensive London artistes gratified fashionable audiences to the dismay of Ifor Ceri who saw his well-intentioned patriotic eisteddfod turned into 'an Anglo-Italian farce'.

But certain developments were to affect the growth of Welsh literature. At Carmarthen, in 1819, Iolo Morganwg (Edward Williams, 1747–1826) introduced the Gorsedd of Bards which was, in the hands of his followers, to concentrate attention on matters not wholly conducive to a serious concern with poetry. We must also note the emergence of the eisteddfod treatise, both Welsh and English, dealing more often than not with subjects of literary, linguistic and historical significance, which sought to make good the want of that scholarly, disciplined investigation of their cultures enjoyed by countries that could boast a national university. And we must particularly note that much of what was composed for these eisteddfodau was published afterwards

16

in such volumes as AWEN DYFED (1822); FFRWYTH
YR AWEN (1823); POWYSION (1821 and 1826); EOS
DYFED (1824); THE GWYNEDDION (1830 and 1839)
and AWENYDDION GWENT A DYFED (1834). For the
first time a public appraisal of a substantial body
of eisteddfod literature was made possible.

Important as the foregoing developments were,
of overriding importance was the emergence
of the *pryddest* – the long, free-metre poem that
was to contest the pre-eminence of the new,
Gwyneddigion-sponsored *awdl* as the pursuit of
the elusive Welsh epic gathered pace. Goronwy
Owen's complaint against the obstructive nature
of many of Dafydd ab Edmwnt's revisions was
met by Iolo Morganwg at Carmarthen in 1819
when he argued, successfully, for the recognition
of a much freer code of metres whose use in
Gwent and Glamorgan pre-dated ab Edmwnt's
twenty-four metres by some centuries. Iolo's
emphasis was on the paramountcy of *cynghanedd*,
as opposed to metre, but his code would also
offer epic-chasing poets what they sought for –
a metre capable of sustaining a long, narrative
line. As we shall see, Iolo's 1819 coup was to bear
fruit in the twentieth century.

The *pryddest* was certainly given a boost when
Alun (the Revd John Blackwell, 1797–1841) composed his famous Elegy on Bishop Heber for the
Denbigh eisteddfod in 1828, and when in 1832, at
Beaumaris, Gwenffrwd (Thomas Lloyd Jones,
1810–34), took the prize for an elegy in blank
verse on Ifor Ceri. The ground gained by the
time the last 'Provincial Eisteddfod' was held at
Cardiff in 1834 is best measured by the fact that

17

two competitions offered prizes for a *pryddest*, one of them to be an unrhymed elegy on Archdeacon Thomas Beynon (1744–1833), president of the Carmarthen Cymreigyddion Society and a staunch supporter of the 'Provincial Eisteddfodau' who had persistently urged the Welsh poets to adopt blank verse in the interests of a more liberal approach to their art.

In 1850, at Rhuddlan Royal Eisteddfod, twenty-five pounds and a Chair Medallion were to be won for a *pryddestawd* on 'Yr Adgyfodiad' (*The Resurrection*), the poets to choose whichever metres best suited their purpose, excluding blank verse. Caledfryn submitted an *awdl*; Ieuan Glan Geirionydd (the Revd Evan Evans, 1795–1855) and Eben Fardd submitted *pryddestau*, both of them having availed themselves of an alexandrine found in Iolo Morganwg's Code of Metres. The unheard-of happened. Ieuan Glan Geirionydd's *pryddest* was declared superior to Caledfryn's *awdl* and consequently took the Chair Medallion.

The strident debate that followed made Welsh poetry, its nature and purpose, a matter of general interest. It was not just a question of traditionalists denying upstart 'pryddestwyr' their right to the Chair. Eben Fardd had attempted a Christian epic, relegated to third place by the adjudicators, but on publication hailed by the literati as a work of distinction far surpassing the pallid, common-sense poem written by Ieuan Glan Geirionydd. There was something sadly amiss with eisteddfod standards when the obvious claims of a superior work were denied. Talk of 'Eisteddfod Reform' filled the air.

Such talk turned to action in September, 1858, when Ab Ithel (the Revd John Williams, 1811–62) and some fellow-clerics contrived to hold an eventful eisteddfod in Llangollen. Completely won over by Iolo Morganwg's druidic vision and fired by a determination to act in accordance with his 'patriotic' interpretation of a splendid Welsh past, Ab Ithel set about making 'Eisteddfod Fawr Llangollen' a memorable one. He did. What matters to us now is what happened to Thomas Stephens (1821–75), the Merthyr Tudful scholar-chemist who in 1848, in one of the spectacular eisteddfodau organized by the Abergavenny Cymreigyddion Society between 1834–53, won the Prince of Wales Prize for a critical essay on 'The Literature of Wales during the twelfth and succeeding centuries'. Published in 1849 as THE LITERATURE OF THE KYMRY it brought Thomas Stephens international recognition as a critic whose methodology was beyond reproach. His book was seen as a seminal work which obviously reflected great credit on the eisteddfod as an agency trying to make good the want of higher education in Wales.

At Llangollen, a prize of twenty pounds and a Silver Star was offered for an essay on 'The discovery of America in the twelfth century by Prince Madoc ab Owain Gwynedd'. It was, of course, a Iolo-inspired subject. Thomas Stephens, in yet another scholarly *tour de force*, demolished the cherished myth, whereupon Ab Ithel pronounced, its merits notwithstanding, that the essay broke with the spirit of the competition. He was not about to reward a debunker, no matter how accomplished.

A scandalized gathering in the Cambrian Tent insisted that Stephens be allowed to argue his case, despite Ab Ithel's attempt to silence him with the aid of a convenient brass band. Stephens won the argument but still lost the prize. Before the eisteddfod was over a meeting of the literati had decided that an annual National Eisteddfod, properly conducted, with due regard for standards was long overdue. In 1861 the first National Eisteddfod proper was held at Aberdare under the auspices of a national body called 'Yr Eisteddfod' whose activities were guided by an elected Council.

In the light of what followed during the reign of 'Yr Eisteddfod' between 1860–8 it is as well that we realize that 'the National' sprang from a concern to encourage a worthier interest in Welsh culture and in particular from a determination to promote the Welsh language and its literature. The constitution drawn up by Gwilym Tawe fully recognized the importance of the poets by granting them privileges considered consonant with the tradition they maintained. By 1868 their role and that of the Welsh language had been greatly curtailed. The president of the Council, the Rector John Griffiths (1820–97), was happy to declare publicly in 1867 that the National Eisteddfod had more pressing matters to deal with than the preservation of the mother tongue: *We cannot afford to spend all our time in the perpetuation of the Welsh language. The language is very well able to take care of itself. I think our time might be better employed than in bolstering up a language that may be of a questionable advantage.*

Those words of withdrawal point up the reality of Welsh literature during the Victorian heyday – and in eisteddfod terms we are speaking essentially about poetry, – narrative prose in any shape or form having been given scant recognition, and drama even less. It is the work of writers who knew that their language had entered a new and rapidly accelerating stage of rejection, who knew that they were not taken seriously as they were not expected to contribute much of value to the elevation of a small, bereft nation frantic with longing for a commendable place in the English imperial sun. At a time when Wales was undergoing tremendous cultural changes, when 'the stuff of poetry' lay thick on all sides, Welsh poets by and large remained within the compound of a 'patriotically' conceived past and a suitably imagined Christian eternity. Modern 'tempest-torn' Wales was best avoided.

Notwithstanding poems in praise of certain exemplary contemporaries or national cornerstones such as 'Y Beibl Cymraeg' (*The Welsh Bible*), 'Pwlpud Cymru' (*The Welsh Pulpit*), 'Y Sabbath yng Nghymru' (*The Sabbath in Wales*), the contemporaneity of Victorian eisteddfod poetry has, primarily, to be sought in the way the past was reconstructed and the future anticipated, and in the way open-ended subjects such as 'Cariad' (*Love*), 'Bywyd' (*Life*), 'Dyn' (*Man*), 'Gobaith' (*Hope*), 'Dedwyddwch' (*Contentment*) and 'Brawdoliaeth Gyffredinol' (*Universal Brotherhood*) invited loosely ruminative treatment. A poetry instinct with the experience of a country increasingly at odds with itself, a poetry relevant to the lives led by the vast majority who flocked to the huge

21

National Eisteddfodau held during the last quarter of the century failed to materialize.

The root cause of the severe loss of confidence that afflicted the poets was the publication in 1847 of the 'Blue Books' describing the educational wants and the moral failings of the Welsh people as observed by three Government-appointed, monoglot English, Anglican Commissioners. Overstepping the brief given them they painted with the help of native witnesses, mostly Anglican, a merciless picture of a populace given to moral laxity, deceit, commercial unsoundness, perjury and general backwardness. Convinced of the accuracy of the charges they had to bring against a people whom they had come to inspect, the Commissioners likewise had no doubts about the source of the national malaise they had to expose. A sour, blinkered Nonconformity wedded to an obscurantist language had brought the Welsh low. The religion of a large majority of the people together with their addiction to their mother tongue wholly accounted for what the Commissioners obviously felt was a degenerate condition.

This historic attack on the Welsh nation's sense of its own worth was of course vigorously resisted. But the damage had been done, the attack had attracted widespread attention and none would suffer more as a consequence than the poets of Wales. The 'Blue Books' were to have a debilitating effect on them. In 1962, Saunders Lewis, in his epoch-making BBC Wales radio lecture on 'The Fate of the Language', properly remarked that the leaders of Welsh culture after

1847 repudiated the charges of immorality but accepted, with varying degrees of reluctance, the case made against the Welsh language. They acknowledged its 'unfitness' for due regard at a time of PROGRESS by according it at best an ancillary position in that 'educational edifice' which they set about erecting from 1870 onwards. Welsh would be 'taught out', brutally where the 'Welsh Not' mentality prevailed, kindly where 'natural feelings' were afforded some room within the timetable. Its slower pace notwithstanding, the second method would of course prove quite as effective as the first.

Education in the post-1847 era was to play a leading part in the creation of a new national image depicting a forward-looking people whose acquisition of the 'imperial tongue' would give them possession of that 'useful' knowledge necessary to serve the needs of Empire. Education would enable 'Gallant Little Wales' to pursue its imperial mission honourably. In the same way, the National Eisteddfod from the 1860s onwards would play its part in projecting an image of a progressive people whose popular culture was no longer 'a thing of the past', dominated by perverse bards whose druidic posturing invited Fleet Street ridicule.

Into the Eisteddfod in 1862 stepped the tireless worker who had already stamped his authority on the educational movements in Wales. Hugh Owen introduced his 'Social Science Section' in Caernarfon and through it channelled utilitarian and positivist modes of thought that boded ill for poetry. A section dedicated to objective, factual,

English language studies and discussions of Welsh wants – educational, moral and material – would inculcate a way of thinking decidedly inimical to Welsh poetry.

Hugh Owen (1804–81) saw his way clearly on the question of language. He was for letting the light of England enter and was sincerely prepared to jettison 'things Welsh' in his quest for English approval of his homeland. From the thoroughly Anglicized laager of his 'Social Science Section' he sought to determine the course of the National Eisteddfod, and to his aid came Dr Thomas Nicholas, a tutor at Carmarthen College and J. B. R. James, a tutor at St John's College, Highbury, both of whom set about the Welsh poets with a will, ridiculing their use of the strict metres and in general downgrading their usefulness *in the face of modern civilization, of iron hardness, and of money-making sharpness* . . .

In the 'Social Science Section' Jeremy Bentham's utilitarian charge, 'All poetry is misrepresentation', and August Comte's positivist insistence that poetry merely reflected man's infant search for truth, discovered another sounding board. The 1860s found the eisteddfod poet beset with doubt, as the words of Eben Fardd and Talhaiarn (John Jones, 1810–69), two of the foremost poets of the time, prove. Both accepted the subservience of their mother tongue and the diminished role of the poet in the steam age. If poetry *per se* was of questionable value, how much more so Welsh poetry, and strict-metre poetry at that. What could be less marketable in an age that equated Englishness with PROGRESS than Welsh

24

poetry? It was galling when Fleet Street taunted Wales with its want of a Shakespeare, a Milton, a Wordsworth or a Tennyson. It was shattering when Matthew Arnold, scourge of philistinism and hawker of 'Celtic magic', insisted that any Welsh poet with anything worth saying should say it in English.

Edward Dafydd, in 1655, expressed the sense of desolation he felt as he pondered the passing of the old order and the coming of a bleak age: 'Nid yw'r byd hwn gyda'r beirdd' *(This world is not for poets)*. He could well have been speaking for the poets of the 1860s. Denied any influence at the centre of things, their poetry occupied areas reserved for a kind of compensatory Welshness. If the material life of Wales was to be given over to the use of English, its spiritual and moral well-being could still be entrusted to the mother tongue. Wales's apologists would use the 'imperial tongue' to prove that the nation's head was clear and 'yr heniaith' to signify that its heart and soul were still inviolate. As Thomas Gee, owner of Y FANER and one of the dominant Welshmen of his era said in 1866 when facing-up to the future of the language, English should have the world, Welsh the inner sanctum. That, too, was exactly how Islwyn (the Revd William Thomas, 1832–78), a poet of undeniable significance, saw the way ahead.

While shunning commercial enterprise, the Welsh language would seek to build a lasting mansion for itself on the firm foundation of sermon and pulpit. To paraphrase Thomas Gee: *Let the foreigner extract the ores within our mountains, we*

*have treasures a thousand times richer in our old language
and our ministry. Let us not yield these to him whatever.*
However, should the struggle prove quite futile
at home there could still be hope in the thousands
emigrating to America. From fortress Snowdonia
to the teeming banks of the Mississippi was but a
short step in Thomas Gee's scenario. From Old
Country to New World to Eternity. What might
providence not have in store for 'yr hen
Gymraeg'?

Eisteddfod poetry after 1847 found itself trapped
within the part allotted the Welsh language in
the counter-attack against the 'Blue Books'. It
would essentially help to promote the image of
a God-fearing, Queen-loving, Empire-supporting,
self-improving, moral, earnest and wholesomely
patriotic people whose National Eisteddfod annually displayed their worth. It would help to
underpin those self-congratulatory labels sported
on all public occasions soon after 1847 – 'Gwlad
y Cymanfaoedd', 'Gwlad y Menyg Gwynion',
'Gwlad y Gân', 'Cymru lân, Cymru lonydd'.
The ridicule which the Gorsedd unfortunately
attracted would be offset by the want of offence
in the poetry produced. That, inevitably, confirmed the order of the day.

Disturbing self-examination was avoided. Welsh
patriotism as an imperial asset was regularly
paraded and Gwalia as the most ruly of Victoria's
territories persistently asked for fair treatment.
Victorian eisteddfod culture reflected the
neuroses of a people ever conscious of the need
to prove themselves to that great neighbour ever
ready to voice disapproval. Rector John Griffiths

caught what was a prevailing concern after 1847 when he confessed at Carmarthen in 1867, in the aftermath of the fulminating attack made on 'all things Welsh' by *The Times* in 1866, that *we are aware that we shall have many eyes upon us, that we shall be scanned narrowly . . . We are aware that there is an annual judgement passed upon us . . .*

That this ongoing fear of inspection lay heavy on the premier cultural institution of Victorian Wales need not be doubted. Equally clear is the price Welsh literature had to pay on its account. Despite a deep awareness of the crisis afflicting the language, not a single poem honestly confronted it. Almost without exception the poets dismissed its enemies as so much chaff, foreseeing for it a limitless future, bright with triumphs scarcely imaginable. Glanffrwd's winning *pryddest* on 'Y Gymraeg' in the London Jubilee Eisteddfod of 1887 was the high point of that kind of bravado. Nevertheless, the most important statement on the language problem was made by Ceiriog in 'Siaradwch y Ddwy' *(Speak Both)*, a short song wedded to a traditional tune in which little Llewelyn was told how best to defuse the issue. He was, quite simply, to refuse to state a preference. The fact that the poem which most directly addressed the language crisis was a popular piece advocating evasion crystallizes the sense of insecurity which lies at the heart of Welsh Victorian literature.

That insecurity accounts for the trifling nature of eisteddfod satire. The Welsh had had their fill of satire in the 'Blue Books' – and did they so wish, the worthies could refer to the Statute of

Gruffudd ap Cynan which forbade the true bard to write satirical verse. Eisteddfod satire to this day remains a wan growth. In the Victorian period it hardly ever amounted to more than ham-fisted moralistic disapprobation. Again, we can see in the perfunctory attention afforded the eisteddfod novel proof of an insecurity issuing in an urge to project a compensatory image of Welshness.

As late as 1900, in a survey of nineteenth-century Wales called TREM AR Y GANRIF, Dyfed (the Revd Evan Rees, 1850–1923), a highly successful *awdlwr*, soon to be Archdruid, saw fit to explain the dearth of Welsh novels as proof of the nation's pursuit of higher things. With hand on heart he declared that *The religion of Wales cannot abide any kind of pretence. That is why it frowns on even the best of novels.* E. G. Millward has conclusively disproved Dyfed's claim. The Welsh press abounded with serial stories, mostly English in origin, and the National Eisteddfod did fitfully attempt to encourage writers of moral fables and historical romances.

What would the Welsh not give for a Walter Scott capable, as Ernest Rhys said in 1893, of giving our *superb national traditions and old poetic imaginations a vogue not only English, but European, – nay, worldwide!* Daniel Owen eventually surfaced from without the Eisteddfod and almost overnight became a national hero. In 1893 a prize was offered at the National Eisteddfod in Pontypridd for a critical essay on his novels and the fact that no one proved worthy of it is perhaps a fitting comment on the lukewarm attitude adopted by 'the National' towards the genre that mattered most to the European literatures in the last century.

As for eisteddfod poetry it had been lumbered, as has already been said, with Goronwy Owen's quest for the epic. When other countries had taken to the novel and the drama as modes far better suited to catch the temper of the times, Wales still pursued 'the one poem' that alone, as the Renaissance had taught, justified a literature's claim to greatness. It was still chasing after it in 1930(!) when the Crown and twenty-five pounds were offered at the Llanelli National Eisteddfod for an *arwrgerdd (heroic poem)* on 'Ben Bowen', a young Treorchy poet of promise who died at the age of twenty-five in 1903 having the previous year been disowned by his chapel for his un-orthodox beliefs!

Mercifully, 1930 did not signal a return of epicitis and a laborious chapter in the history of Welsh literature came to an end – not a moment too soon. When one thinks of the quest for the epic coinciding with the crisis of confidence that beset the Welsh poet after 1847, one begins to understand why so much of nineteenth-century eisteddfod poetry has a sorry look about it. We should not be surprised, let alone derisive, when a dispirited poet following a false trail comes to a dead end.

The Welsh epic refused to materialize. A succession of aspirants rifled the works of the 'authorities' from Homer to Bulmer Lytton in the hope of hitting upon a formula that would take.

Second-division English epic poetry was to prove fatally attractive and as we read the poetry of Llew Llwyfo, Iorwerth Glan Aled, Nicander and Golyddan today we are aware of an alien idiom having its way with their thoughts.

That engaging rogue Llew Llwyfo (Lewis William Lewis, 1831–1901) – singer, choirmaster, journalist, novelist, poet – wrote six eisteddfod epics in a vain attempt to achieve 'the National Epic' that would merit translation into the major literatures. The Arthurian myth, heroes of history such as Caractacus and Llywelyn the Last Prince, biblical giants such as King David – all were grist to his mill. T. Gwynn Jones once heard him say that anyone who could translate a bit of English would not find it difficult to win a National Eisteddfod Crown! The nineteen-year-old Golyddan (John Robert Pryse, 1840–62) wrote his epic poem 'Gwenonwy', at first amounting to 7,000 lines, in English and then translated it into Welsh. The result was less than satisfactory.

To an inflated mode of expression which distanced itself from contemporary Wales must be added an inability to construct a long narrative poem around a central, integrating metaphor. The eisteddfod epic, and likewise the *awdl* and *pryddest*, saw substance in terms of length. Architectonics did not enter into it. Most of the long poems written after 1860 are basically extended metrical essays, as if the poets, in answer to Hugh Owen's 'Social Science Section', wanted to show that they, too, could impart knowledge and practical information with the best.

30

The 1880s and 1890s were sombre decades. Prolixity threatened to engulf 'the National' on occasion as *awdl*, *pryddest*, and full-bodied epic contended for the major honours. Dyfed, who won the 500 dollars and Chair offered for an *awdl* on 'Iesu o Nasareth' at the Columbian Exposition Eisteddfod at Chicago in 1893, was quite put out when the number of lines required was reduced from 3,000 to 2,000. These 'monster poems' wound 'their slow length' through the eisteddfod scene and the rate of progress slowed considerably in the 1890s when 'Y Bardd Newydd' *(The New Poet)*, in the main ministers given to metrical musing about theology, philosophy and metaphysics, began to ask convoluted questions which they did not propose to answer. In an attempt to inject serious thought into Welsh poetry they lost all contact with 'the pleasure principle'. Aiming at profundity they were prone to hit the banal. Poets of all ages, including our own, have been known to do the same.

The reaction when it came was decisive. Writing in Y LLENOR in 1895 O. M. Edwards maintained that the quest for the Welsh epic should be aborted. The venture was indeed bankrupt. The public refused to fund it. So arcane a poetry was of no value to a nation undergoing a great transition in its way of life. The people yearned for a 'song' that would touch the heart and refine feelings. Their taste was for lyrical expressions of genuine emotions. The poet that truly sought to serve his listeners would give them a poetry pure, practical and properly calculated to develop their moral and intellectual talents. The same note was struck by Elphin (Robert Arthur Griffith,

1860–1936) when he addressed the Cymmrodorion Society in 1904. To persist with the quest
for the Welsh epic was to merit the charge of
obscurantism for so long levelled at the nation.

O. M. Edwards (1858–1920) championed two
poets. One was Islwyn whose non-eisteddfod
pryddest, 'Y Storm', written in the early 1850s is
the most significant long poem written during
the Victorian period. The other was John Ceiriog
Hughes (1832–87) whose 'Myfanwy Fychan' (1858)
and 'Alun Mabon' (1861) laid the basis of that
appeal which was to secure for him a place apart
in the affections of his countrymen. Ceiriog responded to that lyrical impulse first made audible
in the poems of Ieuan Glan Geirionydd and
Alun, and his *telynegion* confected of pathos,
hiraeth and hearty British-Welsh patriotism opened
a truly popular front in the war against neo-
classicism.

Having taken it upon himself to project the 'true'
picture of his maligned *gwerin*, O. M. Edwards saw
in Ceiriog an invaluable image-maker. Of him he
said, 'Yn ei gân adnebydd Cymru ei llais ei hun'
(*In his song Wales recognizes her own voice*). That voice
regularly exercised itself in the concert, which
developed from the 'bit part' first given it at
Carmarthen in 1819 to become the main attrac-
tion of eisteddfod proceedings after 1850, and
Ceiriog rode to popularity on the backs of those
traditional Welsh melodies which, arranged by
such as John Thomas (Pencerdd Gwalia) and
Brinley Richards, were to be sung by the leading
soloists of Victorian Wales in a thousand and one
concerts. Wedded with 'yr hen alawon' (*the old*

tunes) his words, fresh with contemporary relevance, were to provide a huge audience with a ready supply of consolatory sentiments. In a way that no other poet of his age could challenge Ceiriog became a necessary figure.

At Carmarthen in 1867 his *pryddest* to 'Syr Rhys ap Tomos' added an attractive figure to the array of national heroes begat by numerous competitions. In 1858 Eben Fardd had laid claim to Victoria as a 'Welsh' Queen in his *awdl* on 'Maes Bosworth'. Ceiriog succeeded in turning Bosworth Field into a personal triumph for Sir Rhys and gave his apotheosis the finishing touch by declaring him to be the true architect of the Tudor dynasty which gave rise to the mighty British Empire. But it was 'Myfanwy Fychan' and 'Alun Mabon' that made Ceiriog a household name. The one took the prize for a 'rhieingerdd' *(love poem)* at the Llangollen eisteddfod. The other took the prize for a 'bugeilgerdd' *(pastoral poem)* at the first National Eisteddfod in 1861. Their reception made both kinds of poems eisteddfod fixtures until the 1920s, long after public interest in them had waned. Their longevity is attributable to Ceiriog's charisma and the National Eisteddfod's belief in their capacity for good.

The assault on Welsh womanhood in the 'Blue Books' of 1847 resulted in a flurry of heavy-handed moralistic activity. 'Merched Cymru' were subjected to a barrage of exhortation by Welshmen intent on securing their country's future reputation and 'Y Wraig Rinweddol' *(The Virtuous Wife)* together with her daughters were set up as models of female rectitude in a spate of admonitory articles, stories, and songs. Ceiriog, on the contrary, chose to present images of Welsh courtship and marriage in tones and colours calculated to attract, placate and confirm. His approach immediately appealed to a wide variety of readers.

'Myfanwy Fychan' purports to tell a love story set in the fourteenth century in which Hywel, a local poet of low estate, wins the high-born Myfanwy who lives in the castle of Dinas Bran. Viewed in its historical context the story is quite silly, but what mattered to those who hailed the poem as a revelation was its presentation of Welsh sweethearts whose conduct was as impeccable as their sentiments were pure. Ceiriog made his lovers fit for a bourgeois parlour setting and substituted playfulness for passion.

One of the adjudicators, Gwalchmai (the Revd Richard Parry, 1803–97), saw in Myfanwy *the prototype of Cambrian loveliness and untarnished honour, such as ever was, and will be in Wales, in spite of libellous Blue Books* . . . The nation concurred with him. Myfanwy became a cherished appellation as Welsh mothers named their daughters after Ceiriog's redemptive heroine who, as yet another admirer insisted in 1888, was *to all Cambrians, the perfection of female loveliness, and will ever remain in the eyes of the People of Wales their ideal of the beautiful of both mind and body.*

That so ordinary a poem, enlivened only by Hywel's declaration of love for Myfanwy, should have elicited such a remarkable response would be baffling were it not for the climate created by the 'Blue Books'. Ceiriog's Myfanwy afforded not so much poetical delight as moral assurance, and the *rhieingerddi*, love-poems retelling stories more or less traditional, which successive National Eisteddfodau called for after 1858 were expected to provide the same service. Essentially cosmetic, they helped to keep the Welsh woman immured within an image which denied her reality the attention it warranted. Safeguarded and domiciled, the heroine of the *rhieingerdd* is the junior member of that pathetic trinity wherein 'Dame Wales' and 'Mam' also shine.

'Alun Mabon' takes us a stage further. This 'pastoral cantata', so described by Ceiriog, tells of a shepherd-cum-farmer who wins Menna Rhen and enjoys a marriage which in popular Victorian style triumphs over adversity to end with Alun's eulogy of the wedding ring. The whole work is rounded off with the well-known 'Aros mae'r mynyddau mawr' which nostalgically accepts the passing of Alun Mabon and his world before greeting optimistically a future in which new shepherds will still coexist with the old language and melodies. It is as if Ceiriog discovered a latter-day noble savage and gave him the role of paterfamilias to fulfil in his mountain retreat. Most certainly, his story could quite as easily be found in any one of the scores of wholesome periodicals got up in England for the benefit of the deserving classes. Not-so-Wild Wales was firmly in touch with civilized living.

Between them, 'Myfanwy Fychan' and 'Alun Mabon' created a kind of Welsh idyll whose psychological significance outweighed its literary

35

value, and it was the continuing need for its particular kind of reassurance as felt by the pilots of Welsh culture that gave both *rhieingerdd* and *bugeilgerdd* such an extended eisteddfod run. Together with the epic, *awdl* and *pryddest* they represent the literary 'kinds' that mattered most. That the effort invested in them yielded disappointing literary returns need not be denied. Neither need their importance as evidence of an unprivileged people's deeply felt need to create a sustaining literature at a time when their belief in themselves had been badly shaken.

As has already been said, a decided want of informed criticism meant that literature poured along the eisteddfod conveyor belt without too close an inspection of the finished article. The two volumes of YR EISTEDDFOD published in 1864 and 1866 fell short of what was required, and while the annual publication of the Eisteddfod TRANSACTIONS after 1880 signalled an important advance in the direction of genuine scrutiny, criticism *per se* was in short supply. However, the appearance of Y GENINEN in 1880 secured for Welsh literature a very important forum in which the function of the Eisteddfod was sometimes examined and its products displayed in 'Y Geninen Eisteddfodol'. Indeed, there is in the periodicals of the second half of the nineteenth century, let alone the weekly press, a huge field of writing about literature waiting to be harvested.

Be that as it may, eisteddfod adjudications left much to be desired and the unwillingness of a man of letters like Dr Lewis Edwards (1809–87),

to support the institution was a great loss as his
TRAETHODAU LLENYDDOL *(Literary Essays)* prove. Dr
Edwards gave the Eisteddfod a wide berth lest he
compromise his Methodism. Again, Creuddynfab
(William Williams, 1814–69), failed to leave his
critical mark to the extent that he would have
wished. A station-master who returned to Wales
from Stalybridge in 1862 to act as the first paid
Secretary of 'Yr Eisteddfod' he was, it seems, too
forthright to be acceptable. In the mid-1850s he
took on Caledfryn, the doyen of adjudicators,
and in Y BARDDONIADUR CYMMREIG subjected his
brand of neo-classicism to the same kind of ruth-
less treatment meted out by Joseph Warton to
Alexander Pope in 1765. After that he was never
short of enemies and what influence he was able
to bring to bear on Welsh literature was primarily
channelled through his protégé, Ceiriog.

Saunders Lewis (1893–1985) argued that the
coming of Romanticism, with its stress on
individuality and its celebration of personality,
destroyed that classical, rules-dominated criticism which Goronwy Owen, by way of the
Gwyneddigion, had made the bedrock of eisteddd-
fod competition. A delimiting criticism, which
enabled Dafydd Ddu Eryri and Caledfryn to
school poets as of old in the correct production
of the literary 'kinds', reigned unchallenged
from 1789 to the 1850s. When the liberating force
of the imagination could no longer be denied,
when sublimity and pathos ended the sway of
reason and common-sense, when *pryddest* and
lyric offered freedom from formal restraint, the
language of prescription was out and the lan-

guage of preference was in. The 'affective fallacy'
ran riot.

It is enough to read the adjudications published
in the TRANSACTIONS to realize how loosely sub-
jective and facile eisteddfod adjudicators could
be. The language of preference could make 'good
taste' fit the need of the day and it would be
pointless to pretend that sectional interests were
not from time to time well served by it. 'Our'
writers, thanks to 'our' adjudicators, sometimes
got away with murder. Hwfa Môn (the Revd
Rowland Williams, 1823–1905), Archdruid extra-
ordinary from 1895–1905, was so intent on
stopping the Methodist 'prifardd' Emrys (the
Revd William Ambrose, 1813–73) winning the
Chair at Carmarthen in 1867 that he actually
'stuffed' additional pieces into the *awdl* on 'Y
Milflwyddiant' *(The Millenium)* composed by his
fellow-Independent minister Gwalchmai which
subsequently took the prize. It was neither the
first nor the last transplant operation to succeed
at the Eisteddfod. More than one surgeon, some
less reverend than others, have grafted their
patients to 'National' eminence from time to
time.

Of those competitions that asked for critical
studies of particular writers, few yielded much
more than earnest confirmations of preconceived
excellence. The need to reassure was always at
work, resulting, as Idris Bell remarked in THE
NATIONALIST, 1908, when he urged 'The Need of
Criticism', in a *reckless scattering of superlatives*. But at
least Elfed's prize-winning appraisal of Ceiriog's
poetry in 1888 pointed in the direction of per-

ceptive criticism. That year, Elfed (the Revd Howell Elvet Lewis, 1860–1953) scooped the pot, taking four of the major prizes at Wrexham – one of them for his *rhieingerdd*, 'Llyn y Morwynion', which is the best of its kind. It was the triumph of a naturally gifted man whose education gave him a head start over his fellow-competitors. It was also a clear indication of what lay in store once the Eisteddfod could start tapping the talents of those privileged young people who from the 1880s onwards would avail themselves of the advantages of a higher education.

What bedevilled nineteenth-century Welsh literature in Saunders Lewis's view was a fear of the truth about man's nature. The nation's peace of mind, as conceived by its cultural leaders, required a nice choice of human experiences for literary treatment. Despite the preponderance of pulpit poets, no religious poetry of note emerged and Dr R. Tudur Jones has marked a reluctance to come to terms with the blood and flesh awfulness of man's fall from grace. SIN became a convenient logo for a literature concerned with proper attitudes.

It should not be thought that the prevailing literary scene went unremarked by the occasional perceptive observer. Writing in 1883, Hawen (the Revd David Adams, 1845–1923) insisted that man, his feelings and his fate, had for far too long been neglected by the poet, and in 1885 Edward Foulkes called for more freedom, daring and honesty in Welsh literature. If the language was to survive as a literary force, the sooner it functioned as a means of transmitting serious thought the better. Such commentators, and they were not alone, were actually reinforcing what Henry Austin Bruce, MP, had said at the first National Eisteddfod in 1861 when he maintained, echoing Alexander Pope's famous dictum about the proper study of mankind, that it was the human heart, *not beautiful scenery, not beautiful rocks or cascades* which should above all else merit the poet's attention.

In the aftermath of the Bangor National Eisteddfod in 1890, Y TRAETHODYDD invited five prominent Welshmen to contribute to a symposium on the Eisteddfod, assessing its present condition and forecasting future developments. Leaving aside the practicalities of running the show, what most gave cause for concern was the pronounced Anglicization of 'the National' by 1890 and its total domination by the musical side. Three of the contributors were very much for reasserting the 'traditional' authority of the Gorsedd of Bards, but Professor John Rhŷs (1840–1915) wished more than anything to reform the system of choosing subjects for the literature competitions.

Rhŷs maintained that a competent committee should determine the subjects for the main prizes which would then be announced two years in advance of the competition. As for the nature of the chosen subjects in poetry, let there be an end to biblical and theological square-bashing. It was high time that the poets rediscovered the glories of the nation's old literature and turned the Mabinogi and the Arthurian romances to good current account. Six years later, at Llandudno, an adjudicator appeared whose positive response, both to the Gorsedd's vaunted authority and the literary treasures of the past would make him a towering presence on the stage of the National Eisteddfod until his death in 1929. Few, in 1896, could have foreseen the significance of the part John Morris-Jones was about to start playing.

The monograph already published in this series obviates any need to enlarge on his career. What he brought to the Eisteddfod was an acute analytic intelligence, an appreciation of lyrical beauty, a passionate concern for the Welsh language and a determination to reject anything that offended his sense of scholarship. As long as he lived to fulfil his role the Eisteddfod would have at its heart – and its throat whenever necessary – an authoritarian figure prepared to defend those standards of language and criticism which alone could ensure the growth of a vital literature. His long and often hilarious battle with the zealots of the Gorsedd is one obvious proof of his enmity towards what he considered to be false practice, a defiling of the wells of cultural history. Similarly, his uncompromising article, 'Swydd y Bardd' (The Poet's Task), later endorsed by the introductory sections of CERDD DAFOD (1925), bore the imprint of a man who knew what he believed in and would use his position to propagate his beliefs whenever possible. From 1900 till his death he adjudicated the Chair competition nineteen times, never failing to impress upon competitors the virtues of concision, clarity, correct grammar and good taste.

41

It needed someone of Morris-Jones's stature to give the perennial urge to 'reform' and 'improve' the Eisteddfod a cutting edge. Where he led, others followed. Throughout this century scores of articles have discussed the merits and demerits of eisteddfod literature. Indeed, one could edit a substantial selection of them that would tell us a great deal about the expectations and disappointments, the joys and disgusts of generations of eisteddfodwyr. Time after time the futility or otherwise of competition-induced literature has been debated. The fitness of adjudicators, the pandering to their known likes by seasoned competitors, the barrenness of legislative criticism, the ingrained conservatism of the eisteddfod set-up, the dearth of *gwerin* writers resulting in a monotonous airing of bourgeois concerns, the ritual rooting-out of 'bad Welsh' – all these and more of the same have occasioned much discussion. That a lot of it has been automatic and fruitless is true. It is equally true that what T. Gwynn Jones, W. J. Gruffydd, R. Williams Parry, T. H. Parry-Williams, Saunders Lewis, Kate Roberts, Gwenallt, G. J. Williams, T. J. Morgan, Thomas Parry, Alun Llewelyn-Williams, D. Tecwyn Lloyd, Islwyn Ffowc Elis, E. G. Millward, Bobi Jones, Dafydd Glyn Jones, John Rowlands and Alan Llwyd have had to say on such issues – to offer a representative sample of twentieth-century eisteddfod-tasters – has helped to encourage a wider and more discerning appreciation of eisteddfod literature.

Viewed against the background of nineteenth-century shortcomings the literature produced

by this century's National Eisteddfod has much
to commend it. The occasional owlish academic
will, naturally, find 'the stuff' less than nourish-
ing for a superior intellect and there will always
be some commentators around, usually of the
etiolated-Welsh variety, who find the whole
thing preposterous. But 'the National', nevertheless, does provide for people whose love of Welsh
literature is not simply a blind addiction to a
language in travail, and if challenged it would
not be too difficult to prepare anthologies of its
poetry and prose that would please readers not
inclined to be easily pleased because of the way
things are at the moment. Despite the vagaries
of competitive literature, despite the erratic
nature of much adjudication, the Welsh language has been used vibrantly in an eisteddfod
context to flesh out an experience or a view of
life with strength enough to fix and hold our
attention.

To claim as much is not to deny that eisteddfod
literature is prone to be repetitive in tone and
content, keeping to the beaten track of well-
trodden Welsh concerns. As a string of adjudications prove, there has long been, presumably in
the interests of public poetry, an over-emphasis
on clarity, on easy communicability resulting in
a reluctance to force the language into testing
situations. Some poets, indeed, would still have
us believe that there is a natural antipathy between *cynghanedd* and urban life, and much nonsense to that effect was heard in 1978 when the
set subject, 'Y Ddinas' *(The City)*, failed to produce
one *awdl* considered worthy of the Chair. It is
one thing to argue that the strict metres cannot

43

convincingly play the tunes of today's fragmented, dissonant society, that they cannot run the scales of the troubled modern consciousness. It is something else again to insist that the *awdl* is of necessity a rural enterprise. To accept that argument is to opt for the dug-out.

Such a prescriptive attitude is depressing when one recalls how T. H. Parry-Williams's *pryddest*, 'Y Ddinas', showed as far back as 1915 how the language could confidently traverse territory formerly considered a no-go area for Welsh poets. (Are we to believe at the end of this century that such territory is *still* a no-go area for the *awdl*?) Again, J. M. Edwards's *pryddest*, 'Peiriannau' *(Machines)*, which won him the Crown in 1941, showed that the language could cope creatively with 'unpromising' material.

These are not the only examples that could be adduced, but they serve to illustrate the point that the essence of style lies in its fitness for its particular role. Aptness matters more than mere fine writing, and had J. M. Edwards (1903–78) and T. H. Parry-Williams (1887–1975), of all people, acknowledged that principle in 1953 Dyfnallt Morgan would have been a very worthy winner of the Crown. His *pryddest*, 'Y Llen' *(The Curtain)*, tells of the demise of Welshness in the valleys of the south-east and does so in a dialect all the more convincing for its shabbiness. To this day 'Y Llen' has lost none of its power to move and petrify. Saunders Lewis recognized it for what it was, but a 'proper' regard for poetry won the day. Sad to say, the *pryddest* that took the Crown in 1953, written by Dilys Cadwaladr (1902–79), the first woman to accomplish the feat, has left no lasting impression.

Inextricably linked with a concern for 'good Welsh' has been a nice regard for sexual morality. The Nonconformist reaction to the indictment of 1847 has had a long run and has claimed one or two notable scalps. In 1926, Gwenallt (D. James Jones, 1899–1968), set teeth on edge because he saw fit in his *awdl*, 'Y Mynach' *(The Monk)*, to speak among other things of carnal desires, but his mastery of the strict metres won him a pardon – and a Chair. In 1928, however, that was not enough to save him from being roundly condemned for dwelling over-long in his *awdl*, 'Y Sant' *(The Saint)*, on his subject's struggle with his libido. John Morris-Jones wrote it off as 'a heap of filth'. Elfed and the Revd J. J. Williams (1869–1954) concurred. Nonconformity had shown its teeth – or perhaps dentures is a more apposite word here. Gwenallt went on to write some of the most lapidary religious verse in the language.

And then we have Harri Gwynn (1913–85) who was four times denied the Crown. What happened to him in 1952 has gone down in eisteddfod history. The set subject was 'Y Creadur' *(The Creature)* and Harri Gwynn's *pryddest*, 'Y Chwilen Ddu' *(The Black Beetle)*, takes us to the prison cell of one awaiting execution for the murder of his sweetheart. A bitter, unsparing, hopeless confessional ensues as the prisoner identifies with the beetle crawling on the floor of his cell in his certainty of life's futility. The Revd Dafydd Jones did not feel it was a poem he could read to his family (the same hoary argument was used by

the prosecution ten years later in the trial of
LADY CHATTERLY'S LOVER) and the former *enfant
terrible*, W. J. Gruffydd, dismissed it as a 'sneer'
against life.

It later transpired that Gruffydd (1881–1954)
thought it was the work of Bobi Jones whose less
than worshipful attitude towards writers of an
earlier generation called for retribution. With
malice aforethought an adjudicator who had
contributed so richly to Welsh literature for half
a century did down a poet who fully deserved to
be crowned. Competition, the world over, is a
bruising affair and in mitigation of his conduct
in 1952 we should note that Gruffydd had spent
a term in the House of Commons from 1943–50!

Since the 1960s 'the flesh' has not occasioned
undue alarm in eisteddfod circles. The Nonconformist ethic has long been in retreat, reverend gentlemen no longer predominate as
adjudicators, the world, indeed, is very much
with us now. It remains to be seen what effect
S4C will have on 'the National' once it seriously
begins to respond to the needs of that voracious
medium which will rapidly degenerate into a
scrofulous condition unless fed a regular diet of
vital language. At a time when AIDS and child
abuse are truly upon us, is 'the National' going
to shelter behind the parapet of good taste? Siôn
Eirian's 'Profiadau Llencyndod' (*Experiences of
Youth*) took the Crown in 1978. One wonders how
some of his recent plays would have fared in
competition. Is 'the National's' stomach too weak
for today's strong meat?

To those who would give affirmative answers to such questions I would simply point out that in the past, despite moral taboos that weighed heavily on competitors and adjudicators alike, important break-throughs were made. Eifion Wyn denounced T. H. Parry-Williams's 'Y Ddinas' in 1915, finding in it nothing but a godless wilderness. His fellow-adjudicators, nevertheless, awarded it the Crown and allowed the notes of modernism to be heard in Welsh. Similarly, despite misgivings, Prosser Rhys (1901–45) was rewarded in 1924 when his *pryddest*, 'Atgof' (*Remembrance*), a series of sonnets telling of homosexual stirrings in adolescent loins, was adjudged worthy of 'the National'. And again, despite the disturbing nature of Caradog Prichard's *pryddestau* between 1927–9 – 'Y Briodas' (*The Wedding*), 'Penyd' (*Penance*), 'Y Gân ni Chanwyd' (*The Unsung Song*) – two of them grimly exploring a sick soul ravaged by madness until driven to suicide, the third starkly admitting the futility of man's quest for perfection, the Crown was not withheld once.

The even tenor of so much eisteddfod literature should not lead us to believe that the institution is essentially an agency for disseminating comforting sentiments to a depressed minority. Were it not for the willingness of too many competitors to strike the right pose in the hope of winning, the Eisteddfod could be a far more effective means of challenging the Welsh reading public. It is for serious-minded writers to extend the frontiers of its literature.

What, then, can be said briefly about the poetry

and prose produced by the three main literature competitions in this century's National Eisteddfod? First of all, some comment needs to be made on the continuing concern to prevent both *awdl* and *pryddest* being fossilized within a layered regard for tradition and literary convention. Since its reappearance in 1789 the *awdl* has been a bone of contention, some of its devotees wishing to free it from the formal restraints placed upon it by Dafydd ab Edmwnt whilst others, equally determined, have insisted on it being true to its 'proper' self.

Basic to the radical argument is an insistence that the *awdl* need not be tied to the traditional strict metres, but that it should always be written, whatever the metre(s) favoured by the poet, in full *cynghanedd (cynghanedd gyflawn)*. *Cynghanedd*, as opposed to metrical form imposed by a fifteenth-century authoritarian, should be the *sine qua non*. Such was the conclusion arrived at as recently as 1978 when a panel of six *prifeirdd* tried, at the behest of the Gorsedd, to resolve the issue. The Chair should be given for a poem in *cynghanedd gyflawn* not exceeding 300 lines. The Crown should be given for a poem or a *dilyniant* (sequence) of poems not in *cynghanedd gyflawn* and not exceeding 300 lines. Metrical freedom allied to concision would, it was argued, be conducive to better work. That conclusion was endorsed by the general meeting of the Gorsedd during the National Eisteddfod of 1978, but it was rejected by those who still saw the *awdl* indissolubly wedded to the strict metres. The debate continues as the Chair competitions of the 1980s prove.

What truly highlights the concern with metre and form in this century – and there is no need to labour the point that such a concern is central to a poet's art – is the response to the coming of *vers libre*. What blank verse was to the nineteenth century, *vers libre* has been to this. In 1925, Wil Ifan (the Revd William Evans, 1882–1968), made an important break-through when his *pryddest* in *vers libre*, 'Bro fy Mebyd' *(My Childhood Home)*, was awarded the Crown. Still more startling was the achievement of Gwyndaf (the Revd Evan Gwyndaf Evans, 1913–87) when he took the Chair in 1935 with a poem in *vers libre* wedded with *cynghanedd*. Things have never been the same since.

Indeed, it has been claimed that Gwyndaf made a nonsense of the distinction between *awdl* and *pryddest*, creating a hybrid that would drive adjudicators to an early grave, and it would seem that the 1978 decision in denying a place for *cynghanedd gyflawn* in the Crown competition was an attempt to restore some semblance of order to a situation that threatened to get out of hand. In 1983, the National Eisteddfod tried to appease those critics who felt that *vers libre* was stifling Welsh lyricism by limiting the Crown competition to poems in regular metre and rhyme, whereupon Eluned Phillips promptly won it using a selection of strict metres stripped of *cynghanedd* to create a poem illustrating, in a dramatic manner, the Welsh involvement in the Malvinas War. A case, indeed, of 'What's sauce for the goose . . .'

Needless to say, the arguments raging around the use of *vers libre* have varied in quality. The pages

of BARDDAS, the official mouthpiece of Cymdei-
thas Cerdd Dafod, have been used both to prose-
cute daft, highly personalized squabbles and
offer genuinely informed and illuminating ex-
positions of contemporary poetry. Particularly
worthy of note is the volume edited by Alan
Llwyd, TRAFOD CERDD DAFOD Y DYDD (1984),
which brings together a number of contributors,
mainly poets, to discuss differing aspects of
modern Welsh prosody. I refer to it here as a
good example of the way in which a serious concern with the validity of eisteddfod poetry can
trigger a wide-ranging discussion of literary
intent and accomplishment outside the competitive arena. It is the kind of book that the
nineteenth-century debate about blank verse
failed to produce. TRAFOD CERDD DAFOD Y DYDD
points to the continuing value of the Eisteddfod
as a prompter of criticism. From time to time the
prospect of competition, like the prospect of
hanging, does concentrate the mind.

What of this century's *awdlau*? Twenty of them
have been published in two collections spanning
the first fifty years, AWDLAU CADEIRIOL DETHOL-
EDIG 1900–1925 (1926) and AWDLAU CADEIRIOL
DETHOLEDIG 1926–1950 (1953). The second half of
the century can already boast another twenty
that would compare favourably with what has
gone before. These poems have excelled and
elicited the most enthusiastic response when they
invoke a patriotic regard for Wales, when they
praise representative figures for their life-
enhancing vigour, when they mourn the loss of
past content, when they revel in the glories of

the natural world and meditate on the order of things.

In 1902, T. Gwynn Jones (1871–1949) gave us 'Ymadawiad Arthur' (*The Passing of Arthur*) and brought back something of the mythopoeic grandeur which John Morris-Jones yearned for. More than that, he made of Bedwyr, the knight charged by Arthur to throw the great sword 'Excalibur' into the lake, a prototype of the twentieth-century Welshman who, from generation to generation, armed only with a vision of his culture's worth, fights for its survival against an all-devouring materialism. Bedwyr, agonizing over the catastrophe which he feared would befall his defenceless country should he obey Arthur's command, is one of the most deeply moving figures in Welsh literature. Denied the security of a matchless weapon, the last tangible proof of Arthur's supernatural strength, he must fight on with only his faith in Arthur's promised return from Afallon to sustain him. He must fight on armed only with an imaginative grasp of the restorative spiritual powers at work in Afallon, armed only with the hope that such powers might one day work their miracle in Wales. The closing couplet of the *awdl* conveys Bedwyr's realization of the burden placed upon him as he returns to the battlefield:

> *Bedwyr yn drist a distaw*
> *At y drin, aeth eto draw.*
>
> (*Bedwyr sad and silent*
> *went back again to do battle.*)

That figure has ever since haunted the pages of
our literature. All who have cared in this century
have been Bedwyr's offspring.

In 1982, T. Gwynn Jones's *tour de force* (and it is
only fair to say that the well-known version of it
is a much revised version of the original) was
matched by Gerallt Lloyd Owen's 'Cilmeri'. This
outstanding *awdl* is a tightly controlled yet passionate recreation of Llywelyn ap Gruffudd's fall
on 11 December 1282, a historical event lent
mythological weight by generations of re-
enactment. But no poet since Gruffudd ab yr
Ynad Coch (*fl.* 1280) has invested the fall of the
Last Prince of Wales with such anguish, has
imaginatively retraced the course of that fateful
day with such dramatic immediacy or projected
the trauma of his defeat with such distinctness.
And certainly no poet of this century has felt
with such intensity the continuing relevance of
Llywelyn's struggle for independence or has
experienced so deeply the shame of his undoing.
It is the remarkable evocation of Llywelyn's
'livingness' today that grips us as we read this
awdl.

The driving power of the verse as Llywelyn gal-
lops through the blinding snow onto a Norman
lance is irresistible. *Cynghanedd* has never been
better used for such a purpose, and it is a measure
of Gerallt Lloyd Owen's mastery that it serves
him equally well in his meditative passages – as
when he remarks on the changelessness of history in a memorable *englyn*:

52

Dydd byr yw pob diwedd byd; anadliad
　　Yw cenhedlaeth hefyd;
　　Nid yw Hanes ond ennyd;
　　A fu ddoe a fydd o hyd.

(Each world's ending is but a brief day
　　A generation, also, a mere intake of breath.
　　History is no more than a moment.
　　What was before will ever be.)

The battle for national survival continues: 'Yr un o hyd yw'r hen wae' *(For ever so the old woe)*, and the poet foresees 'the end' unless the likes of the anonymous eighteen who held the bridge for Llywelyn to the last man come forward to help realize his vision. These alone, Bedwyr's kindred spirits, may stave off the ultimate defeat. Perhaps they will come. Perhaps.

These two poems best represent the mytho-historical *awdlau* which have featured so often in the Chair competition, and they well illustrate what the *awdl* is capable of when poet and subject truly find one another. Further proof of this point is furnished by R. Williams Parry's 'Yr Haf' *(The Summer)*, 1910; J. Lloyd Jones's 'Y Gaeaf' *(The Winter)*, 1922; and Geraint Bowen's 'Moliant i'r Amaethwr' *(In Praise of the Farmer)*, 1946. Such *awdlau* as these, rich alike in form and content, gained both critical acclaim and popular acceptance, and the drawing power of the *awdl* is also attested to by J. J. Williams's 'Y Lloer' *(The Moon)*, 1906; Meuryn's 'Min y Môr' *(The Edge of the Sea)*, 1921 and Gwilym Tilsley's 'Moliant i'r Glöwr' *(In Praise of the Collier)*, 1950. It says much for R. Williams Parry's (1884–1956) seductive use of *cynghanedd* in a Keatsian affirmation of beauty's transcendence of mortality that 'Yr Haf' remains to this day a firm favourite with readers of Welsh poetry. The famous line, 'Marw i fyw mae'r haf o hyd' *(Summer still dies but to live)* has lodged itself beyond remove in their consciousness.

The second half of this century has not seen a falling off in the quality of the *awdl* despite the declining fortunes of the language and the contraction of the audience. Poets of the calibre of T. Llew Jones, Dic Jones, Jâms Niclas, Moses Glyn Jones, Alan Llwyd, Gerallt Lloyd Owen, Donald Evans, Einion Evans, Gwynn ap Gwilym, Ieuan Wyn and Elwyn Edwards have written *awdlau* that would more than hold their own in past company.

In 1966 Dic Jones's 'Cynhaeaf' *(Harvest)* gave great pleasure and he matched that performance in 1976 with 'Gwanwyn' *(Spring)*. His poetic affinity to his subject-matter is striking. His feel for the earth he works, the stock he cares for, the countryside he lives in and for, is profound. The wisdom which nature imparts to him finds classical expression in verse resonant with the power of a long tradition, and his sense of man's eternal pact with the land, his eternal hunger for it, enables him to face the destruction of long-established patterns, the waning of former communal joys, without a disabling bitterness. Dic Jones speaks of the human condition as he has known it, and he tells of the natural world as he has seen it. His popularity is not a reward for mere clarity. It is a recognition of the necessariness of his testimony.

54

It was Alan Llwyd who took the Chair in 1976 as a result of Dic Jones's infringement of certain rules governing competition. He had already triumphed in Rhuthun in 1973 with his 'Llef dros y Lleiafrifoedd' *(A Cry for Minorities)* and his *awdlau* testify to a poet of considerable technical ability. The first two parts of *'Llef dros y Lleiafrifoedd'* address themselves to the afflictions of the people of Northern Ireland and the North American Indians, but it is his vision of his much loved Pen Llŷn at the start of the twenty-second century, its Welshness laid waste, that carries the greatest conviction. Against a bleak, end-of-day seascape an old, forlorn man bitterly reflects on his people's demise, brought about by their truckling to the hordes of tourists whose money, it was claimed, would be their life support. But the in-coming tide engulfed them. The alien came and took possession:

> *Eilliodd wrth fôn briallen*
> *A dileu fy nghenedl hen.*
>
> *(He cut like a razor through the stem of a primrose and obliterated my old nation.)*

As his Crown-winning *pryddest*, 'Y Dref' *(The Town)*, also attests the terror of extinction weighed heavy upon Alan Llwyd in 1973.

At that time it was still possible, whilst admiring his talent for denunciation, to cavil at the old man's pessimism. In 1990, when tourists have been supplanted in our nightmares by hordes of affluent migrants, some of them propelled ever westwards by disgust for a society that has given them the means to act as predators elsewhere, the old man is not so easily dismissed. The Welsh are increasingly in danger of becoming a 'submerged population group' in many parts of north and west Wales. For Alan Llwyd the readiness of his countrymen to succumb to the blandishments of materialism is the root cause of their decline.

Significantly, in 'Gwanwyn', he gives us in his boyhood recollection of his grandfather a *gwerinwr* of elemental stature, hugely industrious and unyielding, at one with his environment, aware and wise. He is the very antithesis of 'Iago Prydderch'. The *awdl* speaks of the inexplicable fusion of opposites at the heart of things, the way in which winter and spring, life and death inhere in one another. To know of such things, as his grandfather would appear to have known, is to live beyond the reach of mere material concerns. To have known such a rooted man is to fear that with his passing things have begun to fall apart. It is for his kind that the old man grieves in the closing section of the 1973 *awdl*.

Whereas Dic Jones's 'Gwanwyn' is a pastoral celebration of man's age-old fruitful relationship with nature, Alan Llwyd's is essentially a lament for a lost springtime, for a glory as seen in his grandfather's life which has now irrevocably passed away from the earth. That conclusion is supported by the sequence of traditional harp verses that won him the Crown, also, in 1976, for yet again his grandfather dominates his meditation on a way of life which he forfeited for a superficial education. A 'puppet of fate', he faces

56

a future without a sure mainstay, with only a recollection of past certitudes to dwell on as he stumbles forward.

Few would deny the right of the *awdlau* already singled out to be looked upon as fitting representatives of their genre. Many others, however, are worthy of extended comment but space denies it them. Emrys Roberts, 'Y Gwyddonydd' (*The Scientist*), 1967; Moses Glyn Jones, 'Y Dewin' (*The Wizard*), 1974 and Donald Evans, 'Y Ffwrnais' (*The Furnace*), 1980, have sought with varying degrees of success to tell of man's scientific curiosity and the threat to civilization posed by the politico-technological debasement of his great gifts. But as yet the modern *awdl* has not assimilated these matters in the way it has succeeded with more traditional ones. It is of the utmost importance that it should persist in the attempt.

In 1969 Jâms Niclas was inspired by Henry Moore's sculptures, 'The Reclining Figure' and 'The Mother and Child', to compose 'Yr Alwad' (*The Call*), a meticulously crafted *awdl* whose formal intricacy serves to highlight the poet's awareness of that glorious web of associations which is the life process. Moved by Moore's sculptures he celebrates woman's fertility, expressing his sense of nature's irresistible procreative forces at work in her. Such *awdlau* are rare. Something of a rarity, too, was Robat Powel's 'Cynefin' (*Habitat*) in 1985. In his evocation of his birthplace, Ebbw Vale, he stood on its head the usual denigration of industry as the despoiler of natural beauty, grieving instead for the destruction of a community whose human worth had been fashioned by industrialization. Not for Robat Powel a pseudo-romantic joy in nature's reclamation of its lost lands, for it signifies for him the political despoliation of the people who shaped his life. His is a 'Cynefin' that the landscape of the *awdl* had long been in need of.

Some fine *awdlau* have distinguished the Chair competition in the 1980s, but viewed in the context of our deepening cultural crisis there is something unnerving in the fact that four of them confront sickness and death. The integrity of the poems mourning the loss of loved ones is beyond doubt, rooted as they are in a deeply felt experience of deprivation. Einion Evans's 'Ynys' (*Island*), 1983, focuses on his daughter's suicide; Gwynn ap Gwilym's 'Y Cwmwl' (*The Cloud*), 1986, centres on his father's long and painful struggle against an illness that eventually struck him down and his, the son's, consequent struggle to come to terms with the ways of a God whom his father, as a minister, had unstintingly served; Ieuan Wyn's 'Llanw a Thrai' (*Ebb and Flow*), 1987, tells of clearing out his grandparents' home and reliving episodes in their vanished past; Elwyn Edwards's 'Storm', 1988, makes us witness with him a mother's death from cancer.

One cannot but view these poems of personal grief in the mirror, also, of that fear of extinction into which so many Welsh writers have been staring since the Second World War. The Thatcher era has intensified the stare and deepened our sense of imminent disaster, so that it has become desperately difficult for anyone wishing to forecast signs of better things to come to write of them with the same kind of passion that vivifies the perception of a treasured way of life going under now. It is not that our poets opt for morbidity. John Gwilym Jones's sick man wins his fight against sickness in 'Y Frwydr' (*The Battle*), 1981; Gwynn ap Gwilym regains faith in a benevolent God and Ieuan Wyn will perpetuate in memory his grandparents' story. It is simply that a positive note struck against the ground bass of our ever-present anxieties seems so thin a sound. The literary expression of our hopes when contrasted with that of our fears is so tentative.

E. G. Millward's PRYDDESTAU DETHOLEDIG 1911–1953, published in 1973, has highlighted the achievements of the Crown competition during the first half of the century. It has already been noted that 'Y Ddinas' in 1915 signalled a significant break-through for eisteddfod poetry. Its impact was so much more dramatic given its proximity to 'Gwerin Cymru', the Revd Crwys Williams's (1875–1968) final apotheosis of that idealized 'folk of Wales' projected with such pride by Welsh apologists during the Victorian heyday. To read these poems side by side is to realize fully how unpleasantly different 'Y Ddinas' would sound to most lovers of Welsh poetry, so different as to blind them to the fact that it was, in a moral sense, an old-fashioned composition. As has been said, Prosser Rhys and Caradog Prichard soon widened the breach made by T. H. Parry-Williams.

If popularity alone were the arbiter of worth the charismatic Cynan (Albert Evans-Jones, 1895–1970) would stand apart, two of his triple Crown successes, 'Mab y Bwthyn' (*The Cottage Boy*) in 1921 and 'Y Dyrfa' (*The Crowd*) in 1931 exciting great applause to the detriment of 'Yr Ynys Unig' (*The Lonely Island*), arguably his most accomplished *pryddest*, which won him the Crown in 1923. 'Y Dyrfa', drawing inspiration from J. C. Squire's 'The Rugger Match', relives the experience of John Roberts, an international rugby wing who chose to go as a missionary to China. On board ship he recalls scoring the match-winning try for Wales against England in Twickenham. Short on rugby know-how, Cynan nevertheless contrived to write a lively poem which, however, did not match 'Mab y Bwthyn' as a show-stopper.

Probably the best-loved *pryddest* of the century, owing much to 'Y Ddinas' and not a little to Masefield, 'Mab y Bwthyn' tells in a gushingly romantic, lyrical style how a young *gwerinwr*, scarred by the horrors of war, turns from the fetid city to seek spiritual renewal in the natural beauty of his home and the love of a pure country girl. A large audience, starved of war literature in Welsh, immediately responded to it and there are still those around who will recite large portions of it to the accompaniment of a good tavern's till. There is in it the ingredients of a spectacular rock opera and to say so is to acknowledge the strength of its lasting appeal.

Closest in spirit to 'Mab y Bwthyn' is 'Rownd yr Horn' which won the Crown for the Revd S. B.

Jones (1894–1966) in 1933. John Masefield again acted as a spur, as did W. J. Gruffydd, too. A young boy, disenchanted with life at home, chances a voyage around the Horn in search of paradise. To reach it he must first fight a battle with the elements and it is the realistic account of that trial which gives 'Rownd yr Horn' its arresting power. The boy returns a man having discovered, not a paradise, but an inner strength and certainty.

The *pryddest* began to face up to the challenge of lives wracked by their experience of the First World War and the ensuing Depression, denied the security of the old ways, driven ever more to question the meaning of things. The subject set for the Crown competition in 1936 was 'Yr Anialwch' *(The Wasteland)*, a subject that but a short time before would have invited biblical treatment. David Jones of Cilfynydd, however, chose to write of pneumoconiosis, the scourge of mining communities in the South, and if his winning poem strikes us now as short of inspiration, the vigour of its intent cannot be denied. Eisteddfod poetry was steeling itself to look honestly in the face of contemporary anguish.

In 1925 Wil Ifan had shown the illusory nature of that inviolate past in which so many poets had sought refuge. His 'Bro fy Mebyd' *(My Childhood Home)* viewed an idyllic childhood through the eyes of a displaced old amnesiac. The final section of the poem is dominated by the pathetic refrain:

> *Dw i ddim yn siŵr o ddim byd, erbyn hyn;*
> *Mae'r mwswg'*
> *Wedi tyfu dros y cyfan i gyd.*
>
> *(I am not sure of anything anymore;*
> *the moss has overgrown everything).*

The very apt use of *vers libre* to screen a fragmented perception of former happiness made 'Bro fy Mebyd' an innovative poem. Its dissolving views of scenes that had for so long been securely fixed in regular lyrics discomfited readers and its place on a short list of important eisteddfod poems is well merited.

It seemed in 1937 and 1944 that J. M. Edwards was intent on reaffirming the steadfast goodness of the old rural life in 'Y Pentref' *(The Village)* and 'Yr Aradr' *(The Plough)*, but in between he had interposed, in 1941, 'Peiriannau' *(Machines)*, a stark warning in *vers libre* that modern man is in danger of being depersonalized and mechanized by industry. A teacher, he had himself left Cardiganshire for Barry in 1935 and from there he observed with dismay the exodus from the country in pursuit of a better return for labour in workshop and factory. J. M. Edwards's three *pryddestau* focus on the same concern – the impoverishment of society as man uproots himself to serve a materialism which cannot make good with cash what it destroys of his humanity. Literature, the world over, has long argued that man needs strong ties with people and place. He needs to belong. That argument, in Welsh, is well served by J. M. Edwards who ranks among the most accomplished poets of this century.

The Second World War, which plumbed new depths of bestiality culminating in the atomic bomb, put the fear of national extinction in a world-wide context. The Welsh, fighting a long battle for cultural survival, found themselves subsumed, as it were, in an universal army. The cry that went up after Nagasaki and Hiroshima, *'We are all survivors now!'*, was easily understood by Welsh writers. And at that point the age-old fight to perpetuate a culture steeped in the Christian tradition was more clearly discerned as the crazed militarism of the superpowers moved the world ever nearer to the abyss. The loss of Welshness now, far from being a sign of PROGRESS, would merely conduce to the spread of that uniformity of mind so beloved of totalitarians everywhere. Such a conviction has served to intensify the fight for the language, for to lose would be to ease the path of those forces that threaten the whole of mankind.

The early 1950s produced three *pryddestau* in which are crystallized the themes that have most exercised the poets of the second half of this century. Notice has already been taken of Dyfnallt Morgan's 'Y Llen', where the funeral of a collier steeped in the old ways occasions the return from the Midlands of a middle-aged former workmate. He then proceeds, in conversation with a fellow-exile, to relate in a threadbare dialect his impressions of the valley community he has left, concluding with the feeling that had gripped him before returning from the funeral that like the old collier just buried he, too, no longer had a place there. The poem ends ironically with a reference to Stalin's death and a com-

ment on the folly of one half of the world not
knowing how the other half lives. The two exiles
depart, promising to meet in the match on
Saturday, 'Os byddwn ni byw' *(Should we still be
alive)*. Heard against the background of the
funeral which signifies the larger death of a
particular culture, and heard against the background of the Cold War, 'Os byddwn ni byw' has
an alarming ring to it.

The Revd Euros Bowen (1904–88) had confronted
the same question in his two closely crafted
pryddestau, 'O'r Dwyrain' *(From the East)* in 1948 and
'Difodiant' *(Extinction)* in 1950. His alliance of
cynghanedd with *vers libre* lent force to his Christian
certainty that in the cosmic struggle between
good and evil the powers of darkness would not
prevail and man, ever ready to destroy his world,
would eventually succumb to his Saviour. Like
J. M. Edwards in 'Peiriannau' and Rhydwen
Williams in 'Yr Arloeswr' *(The Pioneer)*, Euros
Bowen in 'Difodiant' warns modern man of the
approach of Nemesis as his technologically
fuelled hubris threatens to break all bounds. The
risen Christ must be given His rightful place in
the order of things and man must seek anew a
spiritual existence. Euros Bowen is by no means
the only Welsh poet since the Second World War
to supply this answer to post-atomic man's predicament, but the impassioned Christian conviction which informs 'Difodiant' has hardly been
surpassed in subsequent poems.

The third *pryddest*, 'Adfeilion' *(Ruins)*, won the
Crown for T. Glynne Davies (1926–88) in 1951.
Written in *vers libre*, it charts a young man's

struggle, after the death of his sweetheart, to reconcile himself to his loss, to see himself in relation to his true background, and to come to terms with himself. *Hiraeth* is the poem's motive power as it images a rural decline and confronts the fear of death and doomsday. A re-reading of it confirms the deep impression it made on its first appearance and it says much for its innate quality that it has withstood the attention of scores of reciters who in eisteddfodau up and down the land have given their all in an attempt to convey something of its angst.

From differing stylistic angles these three poems caught in their sights those concerns that would most matter from the 1950s on. They proved conclusively that the competitive poem's life expectancy need not be a mere hour's strutting on the stage and that the *pryddest*, in particular, lent itself to a variety of purposes and could create many effects. With the exception, however, of Rhydwen Williams's 'Ffynhonnau' *(Fountains)* in 1964, a vibrant poem in *vers libre* which, after conjuring up images of things past, forecasts a resurgence of Welshness in the Rhondda, the *pryddest* went through a lean period in the late 50s and 60s.

Its fortunes have revived again in the 1980s with Eluned Phillips's 'Clymau' *(Ties)* in 1983, John Roderick Rees's 'Glannau' *(Shores)* in 1985 and T. James Jones's 'Llwch' *(Dust)* in 1986 and 'Ffin' *(Border)* in 1988 striking some rich notes as they tell of suffering, death, the precarious joys of lovers and the suicide, in 'Ffin', of a farmer overcome by milk quotas and a sense of uselessness.

His chilling, vernacular monologue which brings 'Y Llen' to mind confronts us with a man who, like Dafis the minister who drowned himself, cannot carry on. 'Danto 'na'th e'n y diwedd' *(He gave up in the end)*. Viewed as a comment on the eventual outcome of the struggle for Welshness we will soon know how prophetic those words are.

In 1969 the Crown competition took on a new lease of life. A 'Dilyniant o Gerddi' *(Sequence of Poems)* was asked for and Dafydd Rowlands's 'I Gwestiynau fy Mab' *(To my Son's Questions)* ensured an extended run for the innovation. His ten poems in *vers libre*, the chosen medium for most of his successors, too, express a troubled father's need to justify bringing his child into a death-dealing world, and it is a measure of his success that the sequence moves so compellingly through a number of confrontations with man's inhumanity to an affirmation of love, beauty and joy in one's particular human inheritance. The concluding poem, 'Dere fy Mab' *(Come my Son)*, together with the splendid 'Prâg' have fixed this first *dilyniant* firmly in the memory.

From 1969 to 1988 a *dilyniant* has captured the Crown ten times, proving that poets and readers alike have been profitably exercised by the demands it has made of them. Basically, it is an exploration of a subject in a series of interlocking poems, each of which should have the solidity of a finished work, all of which by complementing one another should heighten the impression of seeing the whole subject in the round. A successful *dilyniant* should afford us something of the

66

excitement we feel when looking through a prism.

It is a demanding genre and to date Donald Evans appears to have made the most determined attempt to achieve a high degree of integration in his well-wrought 'Lleisiau' *(Voices)* which won him the Crown in 1980. The three-year-old child grows to man's estate, his experience of life's joys and sorrows made richly intelligible by listening anew to those voices and sounds recorded for him by memory. The sequence closes as his own three-year-old son begins listening to his life unfolding. 'Lleisiau', in common with so much good literature, is an imaginative endorsement of one of mankind's hardest worked clichés, 'We live and learn'.

But we have only to read Bryan Martin Davies's graphic and skilfully constructed sequences, 'Y Golau Caeth' *(The Imprisoned Light)* in 1971 and 'Darluniau ar Gynfas' *(Pictures on a Canvas)* in 1972, or Meirion Evans's sequence of love-poems, some of which are gloriously erotic, in 1979, to realize that Dafydd Rowlands and Donald Evans are far from being alone in their appreciation of what makes for a satisfying *dilyniant*. The innovation has proved its value and has enabled poets to place their concerns in a wider context and to view the world they live in from a greater variety of angles.

Long denied the advantage of an eye-catching ceremonial to impress its worth on a public conditioned to accept the primacy of poetry by Gorsedd Promotions Ltd., prose has been something of a country cousin in the Eisteddfod. Its inferior status still rankles, fifty years after the Prose Medal was first awarded in 1937, and although the ceremony of its presentation has of late, following Prof. Derec Llwyd Morgan's prompting, become more of an event, it still trails far in the wake of the 'Chairing' and 'Crowning'. The poet is not to be upstaged by novelist, short-story writer, diarist, autobiographer, biographer or what have you. All attempts to transfer the Crown from poetry to prose have been forestalled, the poets rallying to the defence of what is 'rightfully' theirs with the cry of '*What we have, we hold*'.

Writing in Y FANER in 1953 on 'Y Babell Lên' (*The Literature Pavilion*), Dr Kate Roberts (1891–1985) bewailed the Eisteddfod's disregard of prose. She resented the take-over of 'Y Babell Lên' by poetry – much of it nondescript. But what especially troubled her was the fact that the Prose Medal, together with prizes for the novel, short story and drama (in part) had been withheld in 1953, as had been the prize for the short story in 1952 and 1951. From this she concluded that there was a serious shortage of Welsh writers *with eyes to see life and write about it in the form of a story or drama* . . . *obviously we have no vision* . . . And the Welsh, far from showing concern, seemed oblivious of the fact. Y Babell Lên' was preoccupied with trivia.

She returned to the attack in 1958 in an article on 'Yr Eisteddfod a'r Nofel.' Acknowledging that 'the National' had since 1880 offered prizes for

fiction of some kind, she maintained that the
novel as such had never been accorded the respect it merited. In keeping with other countries,
Wales, too, needed a wide canvas on which to
project its views of life. Talk of the great Welsh
novel, however, was still premature and the
notion that many a hidden talent merely awaited
a large enough bait to bring it forth had more to
do with wishful thinking than close observation.
It would be best for 'the National' to award the
Prose Medal each year for a novel, a short novel
preferably, as Saunders Lewis had counselled,
which would allow sufficient scope for whatever
experiences an author might care to explore.

Kate Roberts did not have her way. The Prose
Medal competition has maintained its protean
character in its encouragement of novels (long
and short); long short stories; collections of short
stories, or essays, or letters, or articles (literary,
scientific, journalistic, etc.); fictional diaries and
memoirs. It has thrown its net wide and if the
occasional indigestible catch has been taken, not
a few richly satisfying ones have been landed, too.
Most of the successful compositions and not a
few of the unsuccessful ones have been published,
and since 1967 it has been the practice to ensure
that the Medal-winning work is available for sale
on the Eisteddfod field immediately after the
ceremony. Such a development has naturally
added considerably to the competition's reader-
catching potential.

If pressed to catalogue the compositions which
have done most to underwrite the value of the
Prose Medal, short works of fiction would pre-

dominate. Essays by Islwyn Ffowc Elis, CYN OERI'R GWAED, 1951, and by Dafydd Rowlands, YSGRIFAU YR HANNER BARDD, 1972, have been justly acclaimed, and Eigra Lewis Roberts's collection of short stories, Y DRYCH CREULON, 1968, was likewise deservedly praised. But short works of fiction have been the Prose Medal's most impressive guarantors since John Gwilym Jones's Y DEWIS, 1939; Tom Hughes Jones's SGWEIER HAFILA, 1940, and Gwilym R. Jones's Y PURDAN, 1941 made their early appearance after 1937. Y DEWIS, especially, bore the impress of an author particularly adept at probing complex emotional states. His perceptiveness allied with his command of language and structure would soon place him alongside Saunders Lewis as one of Wales's foremost dramatists.

Rhiannon Davies Jones built on this foundation by contributing FY HEN LYFR COWNT in 1960 and LLEIAN LLANLLYR in 1964, two short historical novels which are unmistakably the work of a stylist. She, in turn, has been followed by Emyr Jones, GRYM Y LLI, 1969; Dafydd Ifans, EIRA GWYN YN SALMON, 1974; R. Gerallt Jones, TRIPTYCH, 1977 and CAFFLOGION, 1979; Harri Williams, Y DDAEAR-GRYN FAWR, 1978; T. Wilson Evans, Y PABI COCH, 1983; Meg Elis, CYN DAW'R GAEAF, 1985 and Ray Evans, Y LLYFFANT, 1986 – all of them short novels which between them afford readers insights into historical, contemporary and futuristic human societies. TRIPTYCH has remained fixed in the memory as a powerful metaphor crystallizing the Welsh condition as it makes us participants in a family's struggle to confront the imminent death from cancer of the still young father, a former rugby player of distinction employed as a lecturer in physical education.

The short novel, then, has done well by the Prose Medal. As for the long novel the story is somewhat different. Elena Puw Morgan (1900–73) produced Y GRAITH in 1938, a readable historical novel which was followed in 1971 by Ifor Wyn Williams's GWRES O'R GORLLEWIN, an action-packed historical novel based on the exploits of Gruffudd ap Cynan. Then, in 1976, Marged Pritchard contributed NID MUDAN MO'R MÔR, a well-told story revealing the impact on a small seaside town in north Wales of an English speculator's determination to develop the harbour. Three long novels in fifty years certainly leaves a lot to be desired.

Islwyn Ffowc Elis, whose non-competitive novels in the 1950s were to prove inspirational, has stated that 'the National' only started taking the long novel seriously as recently as 1960. It is certainly worth recalling the fate that befell Kate Roberts's TRAED MEWN CYFFION when she submitted it for adjudication in 1934. Long since recognized as one of the finest novels in the language it had to share the first prize with a patently inferior piece of work, thanks to the adjudicator's shortcomings.

But in the early 1960s young novelists of distinct promise were coming to the fore. Eigra Lewis Roberts, Jane Edwards and John Rowlands produced BRYNHYFRYD (1959), DECHRAU GOFIDIAU (1962) and IEUENCTID YW 'MHECHOD (1964). Aspiring novelists began to respond to eisteddfod competition in increasing numbers and in 1978 the improving status of the novel in 'the National' was emphasized when The Daniel Owen Memorial Prize, funded by HTV and worth £500, was awarded for the first time to Alun Jones whose 'Hirfaen', later published as AC YNA CLYWODD SŴN Y MÔR in 1979, signalled the arrival of a talented writer who proceeded to publish two other novels in quick succession.

Hot on his heels came Aled Islwyn in 1980. He fused the predicament of a young girl suffering from anorexia nervosa with that of Sarah Jacob, the famous 'Fasting Girl' of Victorian Wales to give us in SARAH ARALL a psychological novel whose power to engage and disturb is undeniable. He was to repeat his triumph in 1985 when CADW'R CHWEDLAU'N FYW, in its depiction of the troubled love-life of the central character, Lois, created a fascinating mirror image of Wales between the Investiture in 1969 and the Referendum in 1979. With five novels already to his name, Aled Islwyn is set fair to become something of a rarity – a prolific writer of Welsh novels.

From 1981–3, as if to prove that their talents were not easily bought, would-be novelists left The Daniel Owen Memorial Prize unclaimed. The Eisteddfod authorities were consequently panicked by the lean years into taking a retrogressive step, whereby HTV's money would, for a three-year period starting in 1985, be given to the author of the best novel (so adjudged by a panel of choice readers) published during the year preceding the Eisteddfod. Retaliation was prompt. Eight novels were submitted in 1984, two of which were prizeworthy, five of which deserved to be published.

For his third skilfully constructed historical novel in an engaging series recreating the times of Catrin o Ferain, one of Tudor Wales's most captivating figures, R. Cyril Hughes was awarded the prize. The most exciting talent, however, was revealed in William Owen Roberts's BINGO! which recounts the floundering of a feckless, unemployed actor whose marriage has failed. The author, drawing on his experience of television drama, experimented with narrative techniques and succeeded by so doing in creating more than one Kafkaesque scenario which excites the imagination. What he lacked was a sense of direction. As he has admitted since, his inadequacy as a craftsman proved his undoing in BINGO! Nevertheless, as his subsequent noncompetitive historical novel, Y PLA (1987), has proved he is a gifted writer who is capable, television permitting, of making a vital contribution.

Bearing in mind the novel's precarious situation in literatures which can draw on large resources, both artistic and material, the part played by 'the National' over the last quarter of a century in promoting the cause of the Welsh novel gains in significance. The Daniel Owen Memorial Prize, if its proper function be allowed it, may become the source of a steady supply of novels, the nature of which will be a matter for the author alone to decide. Publishers, too, may be expected to chance their luck not only with the winning entries, but also with those that have been highly recommended. Remuneration and recognition have been meat and drink to writers for centuries, and 'the National' of late has begun to hold out a genuine promise of both to novelists. It could do still more and should start by encouraging HTV to increase its funding of what is now the premier prose competition to £5,000. To its credit HTV has already increased the prize money to £1,000. Cash inducements, we are told, will not guarantee fine results, but it is very likely that they will stimulate abilities that have lain dormant for want of a rewarding target to aim at.

The Eisteddfod, then, has evolved from a medieval testing-ground-cum-house of correction for professional bards and minstrels into a popular festival which annually highlights the literary scene with the aid of the Gorsedd. Lectures and discussions in 'Y Babell Lên', followed by reviews of the 'Cyfansoddiadau a Beirniadaethau' in a variety of publications help to encourage a deeper and more abiding interest in Welsh literature. That 'the National' acts as a means of heightening an awareness of language and literature as humanizing forces which no society can neglect with impunity is not too large a claim to make for it.

Since the Victorian era, admittedly, the 'National Winner' has been rescued from the more ludicrous claims made on behalf of his genius. It is easy to laugh at the besotted rhetoric of that period, but let us remember how starved of respect Welsh literature was for most of the time and how marginal was the role allotted to most

74

writers. The Eisteddfod, with its huge audience, offered both glory and economic reward. It is perfectly understandable, given the circumstances, that the accolade, 'National Winner', should be surrounded with so much hype and sought after so frantically.

Eben Fardd had hoped to see a progression from local to National Eisteddfod level which would mirror the progression in medieval times within the bardic system from *disgybl* to *pencerdd*. His 'National Winner' would have mastered his art. He would be an accomplished craftsman. But before the end of the nineteenth century that idea had been supplanted by another, which afforded the 'National Winner' merely the status of a qualified apprentice. Having mastered the basics of his craft he would proceed, outside the eisteddfod arena, to practise his art and fulfil his promise.

Such was the course advocated by Elfed in 1892 and progressives have supported him ever since, quoting frequently after 1925 one of the ten commandments issued by R. Williams Parry to would-be poets:

Gochelwch gystadlu gormod. Yn groes i'r gwir Gristion, aiff y gwir fardd oddi wrth ei wobr at ei waith.

(Refrain from too much competition. Unlike the true Christian, the true poet goes from his prize to his labours.)

Few would now dissent from a view so neatly expressed, but were it not for the decision taken after 1948 to prevent anyone winning the main

literature prizes more than twice, it is quite certain that the allure of Chair and Crown would
have proved too strong for many a restrained
contestant.

It is particularly interesting to note that W. J.
Gruffydd, whose stormy and often gloomy relationship with 'the National' saw him grow from
a bullish young 'establishment' baiter into the
President of the Eisteddfod Court, never doubted
the institution's capacity for good. As early as
1911 he had high hopes for it:

*With a few reforms, and a few concessions to the spirit of
the age, the Eisteddfod will become one of the most powerful
literary organizations in the world.*

As he explained in 1912, however, that 'powerful
organization' would not be a source of mature
literature:

*The Eisteddfod should be nothing more or less than an
opportunity for a young man of exceptional genius to win his
spurs – to catch the ear of his countrymen, and to give him
confidence (and incidentally pecuniary help) to go forward
towards something very much greater than he has achieved
before.*

It would be a nonsense to argue that 'the
National' in this century has consistently advanced that principle. A shortage of young men
and women of 'exceptional genius' and a spate of
middle-aged winners makes any such argument
untenable. Gwynn ap Gwilym has recently forecast a depressing want of potential Chair winners
in the near future and there would appear to be

little hope of a dramatic change in the situation which has now obtained for some years. The Eisteddfod, for the foreseeable future, will remain the preserve of the middle-aged. On the face of it we have cause for concern, but we can always take comfort in the concept of the 'late developer'. After all, Euros Bowen was a sprightly fifty-year-old when he started writing poetry seriously.

No amount of cynicism can deny the 'National Winner's' hold on the imagination, no matter how quickly the vast majority lose contact with him in reality. The vast audiences who greeted their heroes in the Victorian heyday and the even larger audiences who salute them today in their televised glory are as one in their recognition of figures whose symbolic value frequently outweighs their actual achievement. The occupants of the Chair, the wearers of the Crown and the Prose Medal are essentially reassuring figures in as much as they signify the continuing relevance of the Welsh language as a telling literary medium. They assure us that a language which has been addressing the human condition since the sixth century still retains its potency despite having to endure a long period of house arrest. It was his appreciation of this fact that enabled the Archdruid, Dyfnallt, to comfort a dispirited audience when both Crown and Chair were withheld in 1956.

It is little wonder, then, that their multiple triumphs should secure for Crwys, Dewi Emrys, Cynan and Gwilym R. Jones a special place in the pantheon, or that the few who have accomplished 'the double' of Crown and Chair in the same year – T. H. Parry-Williams in 1912 and 1915; Alan Llwyd in 1973 and 1976; Donald Evans in 1977 and 1980 – should occupy a place apart. Virtuoso performances of that nature are not easily dismissed as mere display, leave alone mere indication of lean years, but by the same token we need not naively hail such feats as incontrovertible proof of transcendent talent.

It can only be a matter of time before some gifted and highly motivated writer 'does the treble'. Had they so wished T. H. Parry-Williams, Gwilym R. Jones and Caradog Prichard could have taken Chair, Crown and Prose Medal at one fell swoop long ago, but they probably lacked the Mark Spitz-like appetite for the task. But happen it will, and when it is done the rhetoric will run deep purple. At such a time, T. H. Parry-Williams's story, gleefully told against himself, will be a godsend.

A relative, from whose back-breaking farm he had travelled to Wrexham in 1912, awaited his return. His first comment was to the effect that the all-conquering poet should immediately seek GRACE. His second, on learning that 'the double' was worth £40 to the winner, was an expression of outraged disbelief: *'Ac mi gwnest nhw i gyd ar dy din!!!' (And you earned them all sitting on your arse!!!)* May all future 'National Winners' be greeted in such a sane fashion.

Bibliography

Since 1883 an annual volume of National Eisteddfod compositions and adjudications has appeared regularly. It provides the basis for any study of Eisteddfod literature. The following anthologies of *awdlau* and *pryddestau* are also basic texts:

Eurys I. Rowlands (golygydd), Awdlau Cadeiriol Detholedig y Ganrif Hon 1900–1925. Argraffiad newydd (Lerpwl, 1959).

Awdlau Cadeiriol Detholedig 1926–1950 (Dinbych, 1953).

E. G. Millward (golygydd), Pryddestau Eisteddfodol Detholedig 1911–1953 (Lerpwl, 1973).

Books

The following provide much information about the growth of the Eisteddfod, together with critical appraisals of its role in Welsh life and its value as a source of literature. Most have comprehensive bibliographies to guide further reading.

Hywel Teifi Edwards, Yr Eisteddfod (Llandysul, 1976).

Hywel Teifi Edwards, Gŵyl Gwalia. Yr Eisteddfod yn Oes Aur Victoria 1858–1868 (Llandysul, 1980).

Idris Foster (golygydd), TWF YR EISTEDDFOD (Abertawe, 1968).

W. J. Gruffydd, NODIADAU GOLYGYDD. Gyda Rhagymadrodd a sylwadau gan T. Robin Chapman (Llandybie, 1986).

Emyr Humphreys, THE TALIESIN TRADITION (London, 1983).

R. T. Jenkins and Helen Ramage, THE HISTORY OF THE HONOURABLE SOCIETY OF CYMMRODORION . . . 1751–1951 (London, 1951).

Bedwyr Lewis Jones, 'YR HEN BERSONIAID LLENGAR' (Dinbych, 1963).

Saunders Lewis, A SCHOOL OF WELSH AUGUSTANS. New Edition (Bath, 1969).

Alan Llwyd (golygydd), TRAFOD CERDD DAFOD Y DYDD (Cyhoeddiadau Barddas, 1984).

Alan Llwyd, BARDDONIAETH Y CHWEDEGAU (Cyhoeddiadau Barddas, 1986).

Dillwyn Miles, THE ROYAL NATIONAL EISTEDDFOD OF WALES (Llandybie, 1978).

Prys Morgan, IOLO MORGANWG. Writers of Wales (Cardiff, 1975).

Prys Morgan, THE EIGHTEENTH-CENTURY RENAISSANCE (Llandybie, 1981).

80

Thomas Parry, JOHN MORRIS-JONES 1864–1929 (Cardiff, 1972).

Gwyn Thomas, THE CAERWYS EISTEDDFODAU (Cardiff, 1968).

Mair Elvet Thomas, AFIAITH YNG NGWENT (Caerdydd, 1978).

G. J. Williams, AGWEDDAU AR HANES DYSG GYMRAEG (golygwyd gan Aneirin Lewis) (Caerdydd, 1969).

Gwyn Williams, AN INTRODUCTION TO WELSH LITERATURE. Writers of Wales (Cardiff, 1978).

Huw Llewelyn Williams, SAFONAU BEIRNIADU BARDDONIAETH YNG NGHYMRU YN Y BEDWAREDD GANRIF AR BYMTHEG (Llundain).

R. Williams Parry, RHYDDIAITH R. WILLIAMS PARRY (Detholiad a olygwyd gan Bedwyr Lewis Jones) (Dinbych, 1974).

Articles

Hywel Teifi Edwards, 'Yr Eisteddfod ac Anrhydedd Gwlad', EISTEDDFOTA (golygwyd gan Alan Llwyd) (Llandybie, 1978).

Islwyn Ffowc Elis, 'Yr Eisteddfod Genedlaethol a'r Nofel Gymraeg', EISTEDDFOTA 2 (golygwyd gan Gwynn ap Gwilym) (Llandybie, 1979).

Alan Llwyd, 'Y Beirniaid Answyddogol', EISTEDDFOTA (golygwyd gan Alan Llwyd) (Llandybie, 1978).

Alan Llwyd, 'W. J. Gruffydd a'r Eisteddfod', EISTEDDFOTA 2 (golygwyd gan Gwynn ap Gwilym) (Llandybie, 1979).

Saunders Lewis, 'Yr Eisteddfod a Beirniadaeth Lenyddol', MEISTRI'R CANRIFOEDD (golygwyd gan R. Geraint Gruffudd) (Caerdydd, 1973).

Saunders Lewis, 'The Essence of Welsh Literature', PRESENTING SAUNDERS LEWIS (edited by Alun R. Jones and Gwyn Thomas) (Cardiff, 1973).

Saunders Lewis, 'Canrif yn Ôl: Eisteddfod Rhuddlan', MEISTRI A'U CREFFT (golygwyd gan Gwynn ap Gwilym) (Caerdydd, 1981).

Thomas Parry, 'Atgofion Beirniad', EISTEDDFOTA (golygwyd gan Alan Llwyd) (Llandybie, 1978).

John Rowlands, 'Y Fedal Ryddiaith 1937–1979', EISTEDDFOTA 3 (golygwyd gan Ifor ap Gwilym) (Llandybie, 1980).

W. D. Williams, 'Y Babell Lên', EISTEDDFOTA (golygwyd gan Alan Llwyd) (Llandybie, 1978).

Acknowledgements

I wish to thank my sister, Mrs Myfi Evans, for producing a splendid typescript from a baffling manuscript, M. Wynn Thomas for passing judgement on the typescript and Meic Stephens for his patience and encouragement.

The Author

Hywel Teifi Edwards was born in Llanddewi Aber-arth, Cardiganshire, and educated at Aberaeron Grammar School and University College, Aberystwyth. After six years spent at Garw Grammar School as Head of the Welsh Department he was appointed Tutor in Welsh Literature in the Department of Extra Mural Studies, University College, Swansea where he remained until 1989 when he was appointed Professor and Head of the Department of Welsh at the same University College. He is particularly interested in Welsh culture during the Victorian era and has concentrated his attention on the National Eisteddfod which provided a large platform for that culture. His publications include YR EISTEDDFOD: CYFROL DDATHLU WYTHGANML-WYDDIANT YR EISTEDDFOD 1176–1976 (1976); GŴYL GWALIA. YR EISTEDDFOD GENEDLAETHOL YN OES AUR VICTORIA, 1858–1868 (1980); CEIRIOG, Cyfres Llên y Llenor (1987) and CODI'R HEN WLAD YN EI HÔL, 1850–1914 (1989).

This Edition,
designed by Jeff Clements,
is set in Monotype Spectrum 12 Didot on 13 point
and printed on Basingwerk Parchment by
Qualitex Printing Limited, Cardiff

It is limited to 1000 copies of which this is

Copy No. 0278

British Library Cataloguing in Publication Data

Edwards, Hywel Teifi

The Eisteddfod. — (Writers of Wales: ISSN 0141-5050).
1. Wales. Eisteddfodau: Eisteddfod Genedlaethol
Frenhinol, Cymru, History
I. Title II. Series
700.79429

ISBN 0–7083–1073–7